Deckchairs II

Four one act plays

Jean McConnell

Samuel French — London
New York - Toronto - Hollywood

Please see page iv for further copyright information.

DECKCHAIRS II

Four one-act plays:

Day Trippers
The Guilt Card
Theatrical Digs
Short Changed

*Other plays by Jean McConnell
published by Samuel French Ltd:*

Deckchairs I
A Lovesome Thing

DAY TRIPPERS

CHARACTERS

Beryl, well-built and confident
Doris, Beryl's friend, less well built, less confident

Scene — a quiet part of the seafront, at a seaside resort
Time — the present

A quiet part of the sea front, at a seaside resort. A sunny day

Sound of seagulls crying

Two empty deckchairs are set C, *facing front. There is a windbreak* R, *with a beachball below it. There is a folding chair, with a beachtowel and a magazine* L

Beryl and Doris enter L. *Beryl is a well-built, confident woman. Doris, her friend, is less well-built and less confident. They are both of an age. They are wearing their best summer holiday outfits and each carries a picnic bag, together with trophies won at a funfair*

Beryl leads the way briskly, looking around. She makes for the deckchairs, puts down her things and starts to settle

Doris hesitates

The sound of the seagulls fades

Beryl (*realizing Doris is hesitating*) It was you who said you fancied a quiet spot, Doris.

Doris Not too quiet.

Beryl Well make up your mind.

Doris (*looking back off stage*) I thought one or two of the others were following.

Beryl Like who?

Doris Like anyone. I mean everybody else has gone the other way.

Beryl Do you want to go the other way then?

Doris Well ——

Beryl Do you?

Doris No, no, Beryl. It's quite nice here. Very clean and secluded and nice. Quite a suntrap.

Beryl Right then. (*She takes off her cardigan and drapes it on the back of her chair*)

Doris (*surveying the beach*) Just a bit quiet.

Beryl Doris!

Doris But I like it. Yes. Do you?

Beryl I'm mad about it. Now can we please settle down?

Doris Yes.

They both arrange their belongings and settle into the deckchairs

Doris sits left of Beryl

Nothing but seagulls.

Beryl Yes! Well, it'll give us a break after all that song and dance at the funfair.

Doris But we always go to the funfair, Beryl. Every year. First place we go to after the coaches arrive.

Beryl No it's not.

Doris Oh no. Toilets, of course.

Beryl Then half an hour's blow along the front ——

Doris Then the funfair.

Beryl No. A sit by the bandstand. Then the funfair.

Doris Not everybody goes to the bandstand.

Beryl It's on offer.

Doris Oh yes, of course. For the quieter ones.

Beryl Should have gone there this year instead of that funfair. You don't find any of the management, the foremen and that go to the funfair.

Doris But it's a laugh. You always say. Gets everyone going. Your very words.

Beryl For some maybe.

Doris I thought you were enjoying it. You usually do.

Beryl Yes, well, that Maidie Emptage turned me right off.

Doris She seemed to do quite the opposite for some.

Beryl You mean the men from the Packaging? They'll go for anything.

Doris I thought you liked Jimmy Sawbridge. He fancies you. You said.

Beryl Oh yes. But I've gone off him long since. Did you see her on that merry-go-round? With that skirt?

Doris She was showing rather a lot of leg.

Beryl Leg? You could see what she'd had for dinner.

Doris Oo, Beryl.

Beryl Sorry.

Doris One of the men from the paint shop won me a coconut.

Beryl Which one?

Doris (*fumbling in her bag*) The biggest one with a tuft sticking up on top.

Beryl No, Doris, which man?

Doris Ivan.

Beryl Oh yes — the big one with the tuft sticking up on top.

Doris holds up the coconut

To the life.

Doris (*giggling*) Oh Beryl!

Doris I love coconuts. And the ones you win at fairs always seem quite the best.

Beryl So they should be, you pay twice as much for them.

Doris (*putting the coconut away*) I saw you go on the Big Dipper with Norbet Norris. Was it hairy?

Beryl We didn't get that far.

Doris Pardon?

Beryl I was joking, Doris. (*Mock prim*) I wouldn't do that sort of thing.

Doris (*seriously*) Oh, me neither.

Beryl (*still kidding*) Not at a funfair.

Doris Not with Norbet Norris.

Beryl gives her a look. But Doris is unaware, as she is preoccupied by taking out a soft drink from her bag and wrestling with the attached plastic straw

Beryl takes the drink from Doris and deals with it, then she hands the drink back to Doris

That coffee stop, first thing, was nice.

Beryl The men went for a beer, what else. Trixie Jarrett too! Slut.

Doris Beryl! She's in the Marketing Office.

Beryl Nuff said. All that carrying on, you'd never think they see each other every day.

Doris Not to chat to, Beryl, do they? I mean they're all working all the time.

Beryl You're joking, of course.

Doris You know what I mean. It's nice to see each other in different surroundings. That's what works outings are for, Beryl. So we can all relax together and have a bit of fun.

Beryl It's a free trip to the coast, I suppose.

Doris And very nice too.

Beryl Mind you, those fellows from Dispatch go a bit far.

Doris (*trying a little joke of her own*) Well they would, wouldn't they? Ha ha. Dispatch, ha ha. (*Her joke falls flat*)

Beryl All that horseplay in the coach. They'll all be at it going back.

Doris Yes. Well, you're so popular, Beryl. A honeypot to the men you are.

Beryl (*not displeased*) Mm. It's not as if I encourage them. I hope you're not implying that, Doris?

Doris Oh, no, nothing like that, Beryl.

Beryl Because actually it's quite a bother. I mean being in demand and that. Other people can feel crowded out.

Doris How do you mean?

Beryl Oh you wouldn't understand, Doris. I mean you don't have the problem.

Doris I don't think I do.

Beryl (*kindly*) That's your trouble, Doris. You come across as straight-laced
  sometimes.

Doris Do I?

Beryl You ought to loosen up a bit. You're only young twice.

Doris Twice?

Beryl First time round you don't appreciate it. Life begins at forty!

Doris Or even later.

*Beryl shoots her a glance. But Doris is innocently rummaging in her picnic
bag*

Beryl Nice to sit by the sea for a bit on our own. Someone or other will track
  us down soon enough.

Doris Nice beach. Nobody about. (*Suddenly anxious*) You don't think
  there's anything wrong with it?

Beryl Such as what? Landmines?

Doris Oo, Beryl! (*She rises and looks around,then moves nervously across
  front R*)

Beryl Whatever are you doing, Doris?

Doris Making sure. You never know do you? They might have been washed
  up from the sea.

Beryl Well that wouldn't be a landmine that would be a seamine, wouldn't
  it!

Doris It could be drums of toxic chemicals.

Beryl For goodness sake, Doris, there would be a notice up if there was
  something dangerous on the beach, it stands to reason.

Doris If it's so safe here, where is everybody? Why is it deserted?

Beryl (*rising*) It is not deserted, Doris. There's a towel over there. And
  there's a beachball. (*She crosses R towards the windbreak and the
  beachball*)

Doris Are you sure?

Beryl No, it's a camouflaged bomb.

Doris Oh!

*Beryl picks up the beachball and throws it at Doris. Doris catches the ball.
Realizing it is a beachball, she throws it back to Beryl*

Beryl It is a beachball, a *beachball* ! There are people somewhere around.
  There has to be.

Doris Where?

Beryl I don't know — gone to get ice-creams — gone to the toilets— buried
  in the sand — I don't know.

Doris (*peering out front*) Do you know, I think you're right. There are probably people lying down there behind those windbreaks. Nearer the water. Probably sunbathing. Yes. There must be. That's all right then.

Beryl Oh good. Can we settle down now?

Doris Yes Beryl.

Beryl We've established the beach is safe?

Doris Yes, Beryl.

Beryl No Portuguese Man o' Wars on the prowl? No oily bladderwrack?

Doris Well, I'm sorry, Beryl. I was thinking of you as well as me. I'm just a cautious person, you know that.

Beryl You are, Doris. Well known for it.

Doris (*sitting*) And I want us to enjoy our day out, Beryl.

Beryl (*sitting*) So do I, Doris. You're right.

They unpack their lunches from the pinic bags. Doris has an assortment of goodies. Beryl has only a small snack

Beryl You've done yourself well. I'm sticking to my diet.

Doris But it's a holiday.

Beryl No good without will-power, you know. What have you got?

Doris See!

Beryl peers into Doris's bag

Doris I brought enough for two.

Beryl Why?

Doris In case someone wanted to share ——

Beryl Such as who?

Doris does not respond

Eh?

Doris Like an egg, Beryl? It's free-range.

Beryl Huh, so it says.

Doris Not as fresh as your organic cousin's, I don't suppose.

Beryl No chance.

Doris They're trying to get them all day-of-lay stamped, you know.

Beryl What?

Doris I heard it on "You and Yours". But they said it wasn't possible with free-range hens because they lay their eggs overnight.

Beryl Who said so?

Doris The Man from the Ministry.

Beryl They do not. They sleep at night like everyone else.

Doris What?

Beryl They perch roosting on a rail and sleep. If they laid an egg it would drop on the floor and break, wouldn't it?

Doris The man said ——

Beryl They lay their eggs in nesting boxes in the afternoon.

Doris Then how come they always say, "morning-gathered" eggs in *Emmerdale Farm*?

Beryl Because they mix them up with mushrooms.

Doris Hens don't lay mushrooms.

Beryl I know that!

Doris Maybe your organic cousin's hens ——

Beryl Don't keep calling him my organic cousin!

Doris Sorry. I mean maybe the Man from the Ministry's hens lay them in the night and roost in the day.

Beryl (*with heavy sarcasm*) You mean like bats.

Doris Bats don't lay eggs! (*Unsure*) Do they?

Beryl gives up. She snatches the egg from Doris. They both tap their eggs on their chairs, then peel the eggs

Doris I was talking to Sam ——

Beryl Security Sam?

Doris No, Foreman Sam ——

Beryl (*alert*) Foreman Sam?

Doris Yes. On the coach.

Beryl Oh? I didn't see you.

Doris Didn't you? You'd gone up the back.

Beryl Oh.

Doris And he stopped by our seat.

Beryl Chatted with you did he?

Doris Yes.

Beryl What about?

Doris I was telling him about my problem.

Beryl What problem?

Doris (*busy with her egg*) You know.

Beryl (*astonished*) You told Sam? How did that come up?

Doris He'd had them too.

Beryl When was that then?

Doris On the coach. I said.

Beryl No Doris, when did he have them?

Doris Last winter. He said he got rid of them very easily, so I asked him how.

Beryl You got very chummy.

Doris They're such a nuisance, Beryl. Sam said, if I'd show him where they were ——

Beryl He said what?

Doris He just wanted to see ——

Beryl Doris! I think you've said enough!

Doris Well, he had to know the location ——

Beryl There's only one location!

Doris No Beryl, mine were on the outside. His were on the inside. In his larder.

Beryl What are you talking about, woman?

Doris Mice, Beryl. My problem with the mice.

Beryl Oh *that* problem.

Doris Of course. What other problem?

Beryl Forget it, Doris.

Doris (*horrified*) Beryl! You didn't imagine... !

Beryl Forget it! Forget it!

Doris is deeply embarrassed. They both eat in silence

Pause

He's a widower.

Doris Who?

Beryl Foreman Sam.

Doris Doesn't mean he can't get mice.

Beryl They don't usually.

Doris Who don't?

Beryl Men who live on their own. Don't usually have enough food around for mice. I mean they're usually being fed by all the merry widows.

Doris Like me, you mean.

Beryl No, not you, Doris. Of course not.

Doris Like you, you mean.

Beryl No, no, no. (*She wipes her mouth coyly*) Mind you, speaking of Sam——

Doris Which one?

Beryl (*crossly*) Foreman Sam! (*Coyly*) He has made certain signs — discreetly, of course. They have to be so careful when they're in a position of authority.

Doris Oh — yes.

Beryl Did you notice he tried to get a seat near us on the coach?

Doris Yes, I did.

Beryl There are a number of women who fancy him, of course.

Doris I suppose so. He is nice ——

Beryl Very tasty. Mature. Bit of a rare vintage, I'd say.

Doris Yes. Has he — er ——

Beryl Spoken? Not yet. I think he's been afraid to make a move because of making some of the others jealous.

Doris Other women, you mean?

Beryl Oh no. Some of the other men. There are several who have — well — got the hots for me — as you know, don't you?

Doris Got what? Oh, oh yes.

Beryl Well that's the point. So does he.

Doris "So does he" what?

Beryl Oh Doris! You're useless! We're talking sex, Doris! *Sex!*

Doris Sh! Beryl! Someone will hear you.

Beryl Who! Honestly Doris, you are the most nimminy-pimminy, primest, priggish prude!

Doris I see. So don't expect another egg.

Beryl Tch! Now she's offended. (*She finishes her snack and then hungrily eyes Doris's picnic*)

Doris, unaware of Beryl, eats grapes. Beryl watches Doris eating, like a hungry dog. Doris takes out some bread from her bag, and begins to throw pieces of the bread out to the seagulls. Beryl looks on jealously; suffering as each piece is thrown. Doris takes a small apple from her picnic and a tissue from her bag

Doris (*beginning to munch*) Doesn't the sea breeze hone your appetite, Beryl? Oh sorry.

Beryl I thought you brought two cream buns.

Doris We ate them on the coach.

Beryl "We"?

Doris I gave one away.

Beryl Who to?

Doris I do not remember. (*She finishes eating her apple, relishing every bite*)

Beryl (*watching the apple disappearing; weakening*) Doris, do you think I could have the core?

Doris There isn't going to be a core. (*She finishes the whole apple and wipes her mouth with the tissue. Then she rummages in her bag*)

Beryl I wonder where the others went to eat? Fish and chip shop, I expect. Then they'll all have giant Whippys. I hope they're sick *before* we start home.

Doris (*relenting*) Oh look, I've found a spare sandwich. (*She hands the sandwich to Beryl*)

Beryl (*seizing it*) You're a star. Bugger the diet. (*She wolfs down the sandwich*)

Doris You've a good figure, Beryl. Everyone says.
Beryl (*pleased*) Do they?
Doris Everyone! They say it all the time.
Beryl Thanks, Doris.
Doris Beryl has such a good figure, they say ——
Beryl Yes, thanks, Doris.

They relax back into their deckchairs

Doris throws the last few crumbs from her picnic to the seagulls

There aren't so many this year.
Doris Seagulls?
Beryl No, Doris, employees on the trip.
Doris There aren't so many employees.
Beryl True. We're being phased out.
Doris Perhaps its just a passing phase, ha ha.
Beryl You say hallo to someone in the morning and they've been made redundant by lunchtime.
Doris And booking a plane to the Bahamas by teatime. Look on the bright side, Beryl. We're supposed to be on a spree.
Beryl You're right.
Doris And they'll always need you, Beryl. You've such a lot to offer.
Beryl (*flattered*) I hope so.
Doris Everyone says. Even the management. I wish I had your personality, Beryl.
Beryl Yes. But you have your points, Doris. When you've had a rinse. Got a bit of blusher on. Really. You look quite pretty some days. Against the light. Joking, Doris, joking. But, you do need to loosen up. Everyone says.
Doris I'll try.
Beryl Here, listen — the boys in Invoicing were telling me about the retirement party for old Harry. (*She starts chuckling*)
Doris Stockroom Harry?
Beryl No, Caretaker Harry.
Doris Ah, but he was getting on a bit.
Beryl Oh yes, ancient. Will you listen! Anyway, they were saying they got him this special surprise present, see. (*She begins to giggle*) Well — they clubbed together and arranged for this gorgeous girl, blonde, hour-glass figure and all that, to show up at his party. Well, she arrived — you know — and she sidles up to old Harry and she says — she says "Happy Retirement, Harry! I'm your very special surprise present from the boys — I'm here to offer you *super sex*!" And old Harry scratched his head and said, "Thanks, I'll take the soup." (*She convulses with laughter*)

Doris (*staring at her blankly; at last*) What sort of soup was it?

Beryl There wasn't any soup, Doris. It was a joke.

Doris Oh. A practical joke.

Beryl It didn't happen at all, Doris!

Doris turns and stares at Beryl. Her look suggests she is seriously worried about her

For crying out loud.

The two women sit silent a moment

The mood passes

Getting warmer.

Doris Tide's on the turn, I think.

Beryl Fancy a paddle?

Doris Not yet. Shouldn't go in too soon after a meal.

Beryl A paddle, Doris. Not swimming the Atlantic.

Doris Some of the others were planning to go for a dip.

Beryl Such as who?

Doris Well, Sam …

Beryl Foreman Sam?

Doris He mentioned something ——

Beryl Oh. Did you hear him say he was a swimmer?

Doris Yes.

Beryl Well, you might guess he does something. I mean he seems very fit for his age.

Doris Well ... yes.

Beryl Hadn't you noticed? You're so unobservant, Doris. I appreciate a good-looking man.

Doris Looks aren't everything, Beryl.

Beryl Oh trust you! You go for the brainy weed, I suppose.

Doris I don't necessarily go for the brainy weed. I'm just saying ——

Beryl That beggars can't be choosers? Never mind, dear. You know we all say you ought to try a dating agency, Doris.

Doris I don't think so.

Beryl There you are, you see. (*Pause*) Did you say Sam was going swimming? (*She searches in her bag and brings out sunglasses and a can of tanning mousse*)

Doris Yes. Well, I think so.

Beryl We should have brought our swim things.

Doris You never know how it's going to turn out.

Beryl True. Still we can have a bit of a sunbathe. (*She slips her shoulder-straps down, puts on the sunglasses, and begins to anoint herself with tanning mousse*) Meet up with the others for tea. (*She squirts a glob of tanning mousse at Doris*)

Doris Yes.

Beryl I tan very easily you know.

Doris Oh, you do, Beryl.

Beryl People are always amazed. When we were on that cruise, Doris, do you remember? The women were really envious. I mean there you were scorched raw.

Doris Well, if you have a fair skin ——

Beryl I was really sorry for you.(*She applies the mousse on herself liberally*)

Doris (*dabbing her arms delicately with the tanning mousse*) Still, I didn't get seasick.

Beryl (*crossly*) Oh go on, rub it in!

Doris No, I wasn't going to mention ——

Beryl Then don't.

Doris No, Beryl. Mind you, it was a pity about the cocktail party.

Beryl Doris!

Doris But you did make up for it, you know you did, winning the fancy dress. You were so clever with those paper doilys. Quite naughty really.

Beryl (*smirking*) Well, why hide your lights under a bushel. (*She pulls her straps down further and her skirt higher*) It's getting really hot. Lovely! (*She lies back in her chair*)

Doris Look at that sailing boat out there.

Beryl (*settling down*) Lovely.

Doris It's scudding along on top of the waves.

Beryl That's good.

Doris A few white horses out to sea.

Beryl Oh?

Doris Yes. Yet there's hardly a breath of air here.

Beryl No.

Pause

Doris Sky's as blue as anything.

Beryl (*growing impatient with Doris*) Well it would be.

Pause

Doris I wonder …

Beryl I'm just going to have a little snooze, Doris. All right?

Doris Oh, yes.

Beryl You won't get offended?

Doris Oh no, no. I'll rest my eyes too, probably.

Beryl Good idea.

Doris Just for a few minutes. (*Pause*) Don't suppose I'll actually go to sleep.

Beryl Have a try.

Doris (*closing her eyes*) I'm not a good sleeper.

Beryl I know.

Doris Some people need less sleep than other people. I wonder why.

Beryl I wonder.

Doris No telling. Some people hardly sleep at all.

Beryl Some people don't get the chance.

Pause

Beryl begins to nod off

Doris She only slept four hours a night — Mrs Thatcher.

Beryl Who?

Doris That must have been really useful for a Prime Minister.

Beryl Doris!

Doris Tell you what, I'll read my magazine. Then I won't disturb you, eh? (*She fishes around in her bag – fruitlessly*) Oh dear. I must have mislaid it. Oh dear. Beryl, I believe there's a magazine over by those towels. Do you think they'd be annoyed if I borrowed it for a minute or two? Beryl? I mean I'd put it straight back. Beryl? Shall I?

Beryl Doris, please! Please!

Doris I'll take that as a "yes". (*She moves L and picks up the magazine from the chair. She comes back to her chair; sits, opens the magazine and scans a page or two*) Oh.

Beryl tenses visibly

Oh ... (*Pause*) Tch ... (*Pause*) Mm.

Beryl (*writhing up, snatching off her sunglasses*) Dorisss! Can't you just *read* it!

Doris It really isn't my cup of tea. I'll put it back. (*She rises*)

Beryl (*clutching at Doris*) No! Read it, woman!

Doris I can't understand it. It's the *Scientific Computing World*.

Beryl Oh God. (*She folds her arms over her head*)

Doris crosses to replace the magazine, then returns to her seat

Doris I'll just enjoy the view. Go back to sleep, Beryl.

Beryl settles again

Long pause

Doris takes in different things. She reacts to a passing fly and to a sandflea on her foot. She empties sand out of her shoe. She finds a pretty shell nearby and offers it to Beryl. Beryl throws the shell over her shoulder and goes back to sleep

(*Becoming aware of a little drama out at sea*) Oh! Look at that windsurfer right out there — Look! Look!
Beryl Eh? What?
Doris Oops! There he goes!
Beryl Doris … !
Doris Sorry, sorry, sorry, but you should have seen ——
Beryl Doris, I am napping. Be quiet.

Pause

Doris (*whispering to herself*) Think I'll put something over my head.

Beryl grinds her teeth. Doris drapes herself with her headscarf

Pause

Phew! Getting really hot. Breezier down where the windbreaks are. (*She peers out front, shielding her eyes with her hand*) Don't get sunstroke, Beryl.

Beryl Mm.

Pause

Doris It's always cooler by the water's edge.
Beryl Mm.

Pause

Doris I think all those people are going swimming now, Beryl.
Beryl (*mumbling, eyes closed*) Wha' popple?
Doris Those people who were behind the windbreaks down by the water. They're all going swimming now.
Beryl Mm. (*She snores*)
Doris Yes. (*Pause*) I think they're some sort of club, Beryl.
Beryl (*not stirring*) Ooah.

Doris Yes. They do seem to be members of a club. (*Pause*) They've all got matching swimwear.

Beryl (*asleep*) Ar.

Doris Yes. (*Pause*) Pale pink.

Beryl Aw.

Pause

Doris No, actually they're not all pale pink, Beryl. Some are sort of brownish pink.

Beryl Aargh.

Doris Not a very attractive colour anyway, Beryl. Really! Makes them look as if they haven't got anything on at all. (*She chuckles. Then she stops short as the realization hits her. She leans forward goggle-eyed. She gives a shriek of horror*) Oh, *gracious*!

Beryl (*starting up in fright*) What's the matter! What is it!

Doris grabs Beryl's arm and points

Beryl (*peering out front; shocked*) Oh my God*! Oh my God*!

Doris Oh Beryl!

Beryl It's a club all right!

Doris Quick Beryl! Quick!

Beryl Quick what?

Doris leaps out of her chair and hides behind it. Beryl follows suit. After a moment they both peer over the tops of their chairs

It was you brought us here.

Doris I did no such thing!

Beryl No wonder it was quiet and secluded.

Doris Do you think they've seen us?

Beryl How would I know!

Doris I wouldn't want to be taken for a peeping Tom.

Beryl Well stop peeping.

Doris I can't help it.

Beryl Nor can I.

Doris Thank goodness they've got their backs turned. (*She alights upon on a new sight*) Oh good heavens!

Beryl I'll never eat kiwi fruit again.

Doris What do you mean? (*Realizing*) Beryl!

Beryl Isn't it an eye-opener?

Doris We really shouldn't be looking.

Beryl No. You know if you didn't know they were starkers, you'd swear some of them had leather tracksuits on. We really shouldn't be looking, Doris.

Doris No. Some of the younger ones are quite all right. I feel dreadful looking like this.

Beryl Yes. When they've all gone off into the water, we must take our chance to sneak away.

Doris Fancy Sam saying he was coming along here.

Beryl Sam? Did he say that?

Doris I'm sure he had no idea it was — you know — this sort of beach.

Beryl Oh really?

Doris Sam would never be a peeping Tom, Beryl.

Beryl Oh really?

Doris What do you keep saying, "Oh really" for?

Beryl I wouldn't put it past him. Men are all alike.

Doris Sam would never do such a thing. He'd never go goggling at the nudists.

Beryl Well we are.

Doris That's different. It's an accident. And just as soon as they've all gone into the sea —— (*She gets an even worse shock*) *Oh my!*

Beryl What? What?

Doris Look, look who's just got up! From behind the yellow windbreak! Can you see him? There — with the black — with the black ——

Beryl Black what?

Doris Black swim cap. Can't you see the man with the black swim cap on his head! Look, look, look!

Beryl Yes, yes, yes — so?

Doris Well, look who it is! Don't you see who it is, Beryl!

Beryl How can I? He's got his back turned!

Doris I know — but nevertheless — it's Sam! *Sam!*

Beryl Foreman Sam?

Doris Of course, Foreman Sam!

Beryl Doris, he's stark naked! How can you possibly tell!

Doris It's Sam I tell you! Sam! I recognize — I recognize——

There is a nasty moment

Beryl I don't think you need go on, Doris. I'll take your word for it. (*She rises*)

Doris (*back-tracking*) I could be mistaken, Beryl. But I'm sure he said he had a black swim cap — to protect his ears.

Beryl Fancy.

Beryl gathers up her possessions, stony-faced. Doris quickly follows suit, with guilty glances at Beryl

Doris Come on Beryl. They've all gone into the sea now. We'd better make our escape.

They move C, *facing front and ready to leave*

Beryl (*heavily sarcastic*) You're sure you don't want to strip off and join them?
Doris No Beryl, of course not!
Beryl You don't want to join your friend Sam, in his birthday suit?
Doris No Beryl!
Beryl All I can say is you might have ironed it for him!
Doris Oh! Don't be unkind.

Beryl nudges Doris towards the exit L. *They begin to exit, clutching their belongings and quarrelling as they go*

Beryl You're a dark horse, Doris, no question. A right little Jezebel ——
Doris Honestly Beryl, one minute I'm a prude, next minute I'm a Jezebel, make up your mind.
Beryl My God, it's always the quiet ones.
Doris I'm sorry. Beryl ——
Beryl And as for that Foreman Sam and his ears ——
Doris Sorry, Beryl.
Beryl Not another word! Do you mind! Not another word!

Beryl and Doris exit

Their voices die away into the distance. The sound of seagulls crying takes over from the voices

The CURTAIN *falls*

THE GUILT CARD

CHARACTERS

Deborah, middle-aged
Marion, her younger sister

Scene — the sea front of a select seaside resort
Time — the present

The sea front of a select seaside resort. A bright day

It is the type of resort where people, with houses on the clifftop above, once owned private beach huts below. These are now mostly in ruins or gone

A folding table, backed by a windbreak, is set c. On the table there is a small ashtray and underneath the table lies a walking stick belonging to Deborah. Two beach chairs are set, one either side of the table. Deborah sits in the chair set R of the table. Her cardigan is draped over the back of the chair. The other chair is empty. A stool, with a picnic basket on top, is set L. There could also be deckchairs, towels, sunhats etc., set R and set L, indicating the private spaces

As the CURTAIN *rises the sound of waves is heard*

Deborah, late middle-age, is dressed in casual summer wear. She is a woman who has made a life's work of needing care and attention from others. Clearly waiting for someone, she shuffles a pack of playing cards. She puts the cards down; takes them up; cuts the pack; gathers them again and then lays them out, as if for a game of patience. Impatiently, she immediately scoops them up again. She looks off stage as if to see someone approaching. She at once begins to shuffle the cards again

Marion enters from UR. *She is dressed in a light town suit and carries a handbag. She is a few years younger than Deborah and has once been very pretty, but is now faded and rather drawn*

The sound of waves fades

Deborah (*looking Marion up and down*) You didn't go up to the house yet then?
Marion No.
Deborah You'll be hot. You've been so long. I felt sure you must have gone back home to *Curlews*.

Marion stands looking intently at Deborah

(*Busy with the cards again*) I would have thought you would have changed. We're going to play cards, aren't we? Marion?
Marion (*at last*) Of course. (*She sits in the empty chair*)

Deborah You'll be very hot. I'm hot. That lemonade would be nice. (*Pause*)
 You did put it in?
Marion (*rising*) Yes, I put it in. (*She crosses to the stool, puts down her
 handbag and opens the basket*)
Deborah In the cold flask?
Marion Yes, Deborah. (*She gets a flask from the basket and takes it to the
 table*)
Deborah (*sweetly*) Beakers!

*Marion crosses back to the basket, gets out two beakers and brings them back
to the table. Deborah tries to unscrew the flask. Marion takes the flask from
Deborah and opens it*

 Why do you always have to screw everything up so tightly. You know how
 my wrists are. Go on then, pour it. Pour it!

Marion pours the lemonade into the two beakers

 (*Peering into her beaker*) Did you use those lemons?
Marion Yes.
Deborah Doesn't look like real lemons. (*She sips*) Are you sure?
Marion I'm sure. (*She fishes in her beaker*) Look there's a pip. OK?
Deborah A pip? You didn't strain it then? Never mind. I'll just have to watch
 out for my teeth, won't I?

*Deborah deals the cards. Marion crosses to the basket and puts the flask
away. She returns to her chair, takes off her jacket, and hangs the jacket over
the back of her chair. She sits. The two women sip their drinks and sort their
playing hands*

Deborah (*looking at Marion with curiosity. At last*) Well?
Marion (*not looking up*) Wait a minute.
Deborah Not the cards, Marion. The doctor.

Marion glances at her

Deborah (*impatiently*) That's where you've been, isn't it?
Marion No, not to the doctor, Deborah.
Deborah Well consultant — consultant. For goodness sake, Marion. So —
 was he satisfied with you?
Marion (*playing a card*) What a funny way to put it.
Deborah Am I supposed to play Twenty Questions? You did see him, didn't
 you?
Marion Mr Pelham, yes.
Deborah And?

Marion Your turn.

Deborah (*slapping down a card*) Tch! Did he say you were better or worse or what?

Marion Worse, though he didn't use the word.

Deborah Worse! Are you sure? Do you feel worse?

Marion does not reply. She studies her cards closely. This card game is one of their own inventing and can be adapted. Mostly, when Marion plays a card, Deborah plays one immediately afterwards, then talks while she waits for Marion who is often not concentrating on the game

I mean they do make mistakes you know. Mix up people's records. It's well known. I didn't say as much to young Dr Collins, of course. But, I did mention that you had always been the strong one — and it seemed very odd to me. Bursting with health you always were. Never a day's illness when you were a baby. Never caught anything at school. That year when everyone was covered in spots — even the teachers — you weren't. Not you! Never an ache or pain with your period. Lucky old Marion.

Marion Well, that was then. (*She plays a card*)

Deborah (*playing a card*) I told him, it doesn't make sense. I said, I know you've lost some weight. But, then you were always quite slight as a girl. Pretty and slim and strong as an ox, that's what Dadda always said. Marion is strong as a ox.

Marion Did he? (*She plays a card and takes another*)

Deborah You know he did. (*Playing a card*) And you were. I told young Dr Collins that I was always the poorly one. Spent half my time in bed with some trouble or other. Do you remember? Marion?

Marion I remember you needed me to tie up your shoes.

Deborah (*sighing*) I know I was a terrible disappointment to Dadda and Mamma. Still they had better luck next time. With you. I told young Dr Collins that after Mamma passed on, Dadda and I both relied on you. Dadda said you were a ray of sunshine. You were his favourite …

Marion No, you were his favourite, Deborah.

Deborah I don't see how you can say that. He always pretended I was, I'll grant you. That was because of my disability ——

Marion (*sharply*) Let's give it a rest.

Deborah reacts to Marion's tone of voice with a hard stare. But Marion is studying her cards. They play silently for a moment

Deborah (*laying some cards*) Running one spades. I told young Dr Collins, Dadda always said I wasn't likely to have much of a life, so he wanted to make things as easy for me as he could. He told everyone. Well, you know ——

Marion (*quietly*) Yes, I know.

Deborah "We must take care of Deborah," he said. "She's not likely to get married and have a home of her own and children. Not like ——"

Marion Not like me. Funny that. (*She plays a card*)

Deborah Well you did get married, what are you talking about? (*She plays a card*)

Marion So I did.

Deborah I told young Dr Collins, Dadda said, "I must leave Deborah happy and secure after I'm gone."

Marion Well you are, aren't you?

Deborah What? But I told him, Dadda got very confused towards the end. That's what we thought.

Marion That's what we thought.

Deborah He agreed that Dadda must have been confused to do what he did. On the other hand ——

Marion Deborah, can we just play cards? Running three. (*She plays a card*)

Deborah Will you listen! On the other hand he agreed it could have been a mistake by the lawyers. It's well known, legal papers get muddled up. And medical papers get muddled up too. This is what I'm saying. I'll bet that's what's happened to yours. They're mistaking you for someone else with the same name. There must be thousands of Browns. (*She plays a card*)

Marion He had the results of my test ——

Deborah There you are! The wrong ones have come back. You read it in the papers all the time.

Marion I wish you were right, Deborah. But I don't think you are. (*She plays a card*)

Deborah (*playing a card*) There you go, looking on the black side! I was told about a woman who happened to see a report in her medical file — she rifled through it while the doctor was out of the room — it was a new doctor, you see — and it said she was a hysterical depressive. She nearly had a fit. There it was: Mrs Kate Rigby. This woman is a hysterical depressive. Then she saw the date. It was 1961. And she wasn't even married then, so it wasn't her name. It was somebody else's file. It happens all the time.

Marion I doubt it. Mr Pelham is a man I trust.

Deborah Trust! Well don't make it sound as if he's signed your death warrant. Your trouble, Marion, is you're too gullible. You have never been very astute.

Marion You may be right.

They play in silence for a moment

Deborah Running two clubs! (*She slaps down a card*) Those professional people like to string you along, so that they can rake in their fat fees year in, year out.

Marion plays a card

Clubs, Marion! When are you to see him again?

Marion In a fortnight's time. (*She replaces the card with another one*)

Deborah (*playing a card*) What did I say!

Marion Or sooner if I need to.

Deborah Why should you? He's on to a good thing, isn't he? He'll have you dancing into town every five minutes for appointments.

Marion I don't think there will be so many.

Deborah Well, good.

Marion He explained to me what was happening. He said ——

Deborah Please! Don't go into any gory details. You know that sort of thing upsets me. Did he give you some different medication?

Marion I think so.

Deborah Ah. There then.

They play in silence again

I think I could do with a biscuit.

Marion rises and crosses to the picnic basket. She takes a plastic box filled with biscuits and offers them to Deborah. Deborah takes a biscuit, gives it a small bite, puts it aside, and then concentrates on her cards once more. Marion replaces the box and returns to her seat

As soon as Marion is reseated Deborah holds up her beaker and waggles it. Marion rises again, fetches the flask and pours Deborah some more lemonade. She crosses back to the basket, to replace the flask

Marion (*putting the flask away*) Deborah, Mr Pelham said I must ease up a bit. Actually, I've had to already, I told him ——

Deborah Oh I had all that from young Dr Collins! That house is too much for your sister to manage. Get more help — it's too big. *Curlews* too big! *Curlews* is the finest Georgian house for miles around! (*Gesturing*) Perched up there above us, looking out to sea — dominating the east cliff. It's perfectly situated and it's perfectly proportioned.

Marion (*looking up at the cliff top*) It seems larger lately. (*She returns to her seat*)

Deborah What a silly thing to say. You never did appreciate it. You'd have been perfectly happy to live in some bungalow. With that Donald McKechnie.

Marion Yes, I would have. (*She sorts her cards*)

Deborah It was certainly all he could have afforded!

Marion That's not true. But it wouldn't have mattered. When you're first
    married ... (*She lays down a card*) When you ——
Deborah What sort of card is that?
Marion Sorry. (*She replaces the card*)
Deborah He was quick enough to move into *Curlews*. Pity he didn't stick
    by you!
Marion Pity I didn't stick by him.
Deborah That's an odd remark.
Marion He gave me the choice.
Deborah What choice?
Marion A choice of duties, Deborah. To you or to him.
Deborah That's not a nice way to put it!
Marion He didn't know us well enough.
Deborah That's right!
Marion (*quietly*) He didn't know me well enough.
Deborah He never understood our situation. But it's ancient history.
Marion I didn't bring it up.

*They play a few cards quickly. Deborah sweeps up all the cards, shuffles them
and deals a few each. They stop playing cards for a while*

Deborah No-one will ever know the shock I got. You weren't here ——
Marion I was on my honeymoon, Deborah.
Deborah I remember old Dr Collins the day I collapsed. He was very kind.
    He could hardly believe Dadda would do it to me. "*Curlews* should have
    been yours, Miss Brown", he said, "and your sister should be here at this
    moment." I said, " She's not due back for ages! She's in the Azores."
Marion On her honeymoon.
Deborah I wouldn't let him send for you, Marion. I let you enjoy your
    holiday.
Marion Honeymoon!
Deborah And you didn't seem in the least surprised when I told you what
    had happened. Nor pleased, nor grateful.
Marion I was stunned. And I wasn't pleased or grateful. How could I be?
Deborah I would have been!
Marion That was the point! I knew somehow Dadda had got it the wrong
    way round.
Deborah You didn't need *Curlews*!
Marion No, I didn't need it.
Deborah You never cared for it as I did!
Marion I'm not sure of that. Then. I don't now.
Deborah What?
Marion Nothing.

Deborah It was a terrible thing!

Marion Yes. And I believed Dadda was gaga to make a will like that. But, you can't say I didn't make it up to you.

Deborah Letting me stay on with you at *Curlews*?

Marion I could hardly throw you out. You knew that. I thought Donald would realize …

Deborah Well, he didn't. He begrudged everything you did for me! But he was happy to live in the big house, wasn't he?

Marion No, he wasn't, Deborah. He didn't want me to spend so much time looking after you.

Deborah There you are you see!

Marion He didn't think you needed half of it.

Deborah He was jealous because you weren't dancing attendance on him all the time, that's what!

Marion (*angrily*) He wasn't like that! He wasn't like that. (*She crosses to her handbag. She takes out a cigarette and lights it. Collecting herself*) Do you know what he said before he left? He said, "your sister is playing the guilt card." "There's something wrong", he said, "but it's not with your sister. She's a winner." (*She crosses back to the table*) He gave me an ultimatum. Either we could put you in a home ——

Deborah (*outraged*) What!

Marion Well, you couldn't take care of yourself could you? You said it constantly. Or we should give you the house with a nurse and housekeeper to look after you. And he and I would go off by ourselves. Leave you to it.

Deborah As if you would.

Marion Quite. As if I would. Otherwise — the other option was — well you know—— (*She sits*)

Deborah I know he was a bad egg! Ff! My leg's gone to sleep. Those cramp pills are useless! (*She rubs at her leg, gasping with pain*)

During Marion's next speech, Deborah rises and turns us. *Whilst holding on to the back of her chair, she flexes her knee*

Marion He just didn't know the way we'd always lived. How could he understand how I felt. If you've been told, all your life, you were the lucky one, the one with all the advantages, and you've believed it —— (*Half to herself*) Then just when you think the luck is evening out and you can get a life of your own, with a clear conscience, all of a sudden you find yourself the winner again — and what's worse, at the other's expense ... What can you do? What can you do?

Deborah (*sitting*) What? (*Briskly*) I don't know what you're mumbling on about. (*She sorts her cards and plays*) What's your card? Marion!

Marion (*sorting her cards*) Sorry. Running five. (*She lays some cards*)

Deborah (*playing a card and then taking another*) You are tiresome today. That doctor — consultant — clearly upset you. You'll have to get a second opinion. We'll ring young Dr Collins when we go up to *Curlews*.

Marion smiles wryly and plays a card. Deborah slaps down several more cards triumphantly, then pushes them all across to Marion

Marion (*picking up the cards and shuffling them intermittently*) I don't blame you, Deborah.

Deborah What?

Marion It was Mamma's fault at first, then Dadda carried it on. Whenever anyone had some good fortune and you didn't, then it had to be made up to you. "We must make it up to Deborah." I heard that hissed from my earliest years. When I won that RSPCA essay prize and you didn't. "We must make it up to Deborah." When I got into the Grammar School and you didn't. "We must make it up to Deborah." When I achieved anything at all and you never did ——

Deborah Well, I was at a disadvantage.

Marion No, Deborah, you were just lazy. Your disadvantage was you were bone idle.

Deborah What a thing to say!

Marion (*dealing a few cards*) I know it and you know it. Why didn't the parents see it, I wonder. They didn't do you a favour, Deborah. You had as good a brain as me. Probably better. You were certainly more — what was it? — astute.

Deborah I couldn't keep up. I needed support.

Marion (*slapping the pack down*) What rubbish! Oh people were sorry for you, because they were invited to be. Dadda and Mamma ruined you, Deborah. We all had to make excuses when you did something mean or rotten. And we all had to make allowances. For what? For what?

Deborah For my disability!

Marion (*sorting her playing hand*) Deborah, people have won through with far worse problems. Serious handicaps. The real thing, Deborah. Not like you.

Deborah Why are you being so horrible? I was frail and weak. I was premature. I weighed three pounds born. Mamma had a very bad time with me. I had to be taken great care of. I was different. You could look after yourself.

Marion And look after you too ! It got to be a habit. My responsibility. It wasn't fair you know.

Deborah I never realized I was such a burden. I never asked you to look after me. It was your decision. You could have gone off with your Donald McKechnie. You could have gone off any time since.

Marion How could I? After the injustice you'd been done. As you said over and over again.

Deborah Dadda broke his promise. I'll never get over that. All through he said *Curlews* would be mine. You'd get Mamma's money. But *Curlews* would be my home, my sanctuary for ever. Give me peace of mind.

Marion Yes, all right, Deborah. You're not talking to young Dr Collins now.

Deborah It was cruel of Dadda to deceive me like that!

Marion (*pointedly*) And so very unlike him.

Deborah meets Marion's eyes briefly, then sorts her cards

You know, I never remember Dadda ever breaking a promise before. Oh, except once: he promised to dance at my wedding — and he didn't — but I know he would have.

Deborah For goodness sake, he was ill by then. (*She plays a card*)

Marion Yes. I didn't realize how ill.

Deborah You were never very observant.

Marion You're right, of course.

They play on

Yes. It was so out of character for him.

Deborah Yes, well, as we know. He was confused. He must have made some changes to his will and accidentally got it wrong.

Marion You don't think it was intended then?

Deborah Of course not! We know that perfectly well.

Marion Yes we do. I was certainly not meant to inherit *Curlews*.

Deborah It was the shock ——

Marion It was a shock for me too, Deborah!

Deborah You never liked the house!

They stop playing cards

Marion It was the guilt. It bore into me. Your distress, those tears, the dreadful things you said about Dadda. How was I to make it up to you? We were back to childhood. I'd got the prize. You had to be placated.

Deborah Placated? You mean compensated.

Marion Compensated then. Dadda had let you down and I must pick up the pieces. Kiss it better.

Deborah Why are you bringing all this up today? It's that doctor — consultant — he's frightened you. Made you feel sorry for yourself.

Marion Yes. Both, actually. Frightened and sorry for myself. Quite an indulgence that. But maybe justified. Then I started feeling worried about you.

Deborah Do you think you'll have to go into hospital or something?
Marion Very likely. I don't know.
Deborah You don't need to be frightened of hospitals, Marion. The nurses
are sweet. When I had my tonsils out, and when I had my wart removed,
and that suspected heart attack... You're lucky you've never had to go to
hospital like I have. That's why it's strange to you. But ——
Marion It's not the hospital... I began to think what might happen to you if
I — wasn't around. I began to wonder whether all our affairs were in order.
Deborah Oh don't, Marion. You are being depressing. What an idea. (*She
attends to her cards*)
Marion I know I've never been very business-like.
Deborah (*with a little laugh*) That's true.
Marion And I realize I should have been.
Deborah Well don't go on about it now.

*Deborah plays a card, waits until Marion has laid a card and then lays
another. Marion studies her hand carefully, lays a card and looks searchingly
at Deborah*

I think we ought to go up to the house when we've finished this hand.
Marion Why?
Deborah Why? Because it's not as warm here as it was. Pity our beach hut
got blown down.
Marion Was the beach hut in the will?
Deborah What?
Marion The beach hut. Did Dadda mention it in his will?
Deborah Oh what does it matter, Marion. The beach hut blew down. It's
gone. They all went in that gale, do you remember? You should have
replaced it. Some people did. (*She points off*) They're rather smart, the new
ones, don't you think? We shouldn't always have to borrow Mr Seagrim's.
Marion What do you mean *I* should have replaced it?
Deborah Not that he objects. If you ask me he rather fancies women
stripping off in his hut. Wouldn't be surprised if he goes in there afterwards
and has a good sniff ——
Marion Deborah, what do you mean *I* should have replaced it?
Deborah What? (*Crossly*) All right, "we" should have replaced it. What is
the matter with you!
Marion Don't you mean "you" should have replaced it?
Deborah (*glancing at Marion again*) Oh for goodness sake!

They play a few cards very quickly

(*Throwing down a final card*) Mine! (*She sweeps all the remaining cards
together*) Look, I'm getting rather cold. Do start packing up, Marion.

Aren't you getting cold? You don't want to get a chill on top of — whatever it is you've got wrong with you. Perhaps if you'd taken more care of yourself. (*She gropes for her cardigan*)

Marion (*rising*) Yes, I should have cared more for myself. (*Automatically she helps Deborah*)

Deborah Well, don't get maudlin, please. You always look on the dark side. You're such a worrier. I don't know what gets into you sometimes. (*She pats Marion's hand*)

Marion I suppose that's what got into me today. Worrying about the future. Well, your future.

During the following dialogue, Marion packs the cards into their case and crosses to the picnic basket to put the cards away. Then she returns to the table, collects the ashtray from the table and returns to the basket. She finds a plastic bag, empties the contents of the ashtray into it and packs both the bag and the ashtray away

Deborah I shall have a word with young Dr Collins. Those consultants take too much on themselves, filling you with all these fears — probably half of them unfounded. It's too bad. I'll say, "Marion was frightened half to death." I suppose you wandered about the town with everything going round in your mind.

Marion Yes I did. But that was later.

Deborah What?

Marion That was afterwards.

Deborah You've lost me now. Are you saying you went off somewhere else before coming home?

Marion Yes.

Deborah Well, where? To another doctor? Did that consultant send you to some clinic or other? I thought you'd been a long time. I thought you'd gone shopping.

Marion No. I didn't forget you were waiting for me.

Deborah I thought you'd gone gallivanting around the town.

Marion I wasn't gallivanting, Deborah.

Deborah I realize that now.

Marion After what I'd been told, I sat on a bench in a square for a while. As you say, I'm a worrier. And I cast my mind back. And I remembered what had happened about Dadda's will. And I remembered I had never made a will myself. You always said it wasn't necessary because you were my next-of-kin.

Deborah That's perfectly right, Marion. What is all this about?

Marion (*moving to lean on her chair*) It's about my being businesslike for once. Curiously enough, I was thinking along your lines. About how documents can get misplaced, muddled up and all that. That's what you said, wasn't it?

Deborah (*ignoring the question*) There's a very black cloud out there at sea. We'll get caught in a shower if we hang about here.

Marion I thought, what if something went terribly wrong again; after I was dead. Like it did with Dadda. What if, for some reason, *Curlews* went to Donald McKechnie. Can a divorced husband be a next-of-kin? I didn't know.

Deborah I can tell you categorically he wouldn't get *Curlews*!

Marion No. (*She turns and confronts Deborah*) Any more than I did!

A long pause

Deborah is very still

Marion (*crossing to collect beakers*) Funny, in all these years, I've never had occasion to make contact with our solicitors. Sedgewick and Porlock. Yes. Sedgewick and Porlock and Partners. The partners don't seem to have their own names. Rather nice old offices, aren't they?

Deborah I don't know. I ——

Marion (*crossing to the picnic basket*) Don't you remember? I mean, you've been there, haven't you? Sedgewick and Porlock and Partners. I hadn't, of course. I had quite a task finding them. I met a Mr Bainbridge. I asked for Mr Sedgewick but he's dead. So is Mr Porlock. But Mr Bainbridge was very kind. When I said who I was, he looked out the papers for me. (*She puts the beakers into the basket*)

Deborah The papers ?

Marion I wanted to make sure everything was in order. I wanted to make a will of my own and make you the beneficiary. Make absolutely certain that you would inherit *Curlews* this time. I explained to Mr Bainbridge that the consultant had been quite forthright with me about my state of health. Been quite straight about my expectations. I'd asked him to be honest. I've always valued honesty. I think that was what had troubled me most about Dadda, all those years ago. Believing he had been dishonest about his intentions.

Deborah Marion...

Marion Yes?

Deborah Never mind.

Marion (*closing in on Deborah*) Don't you want to know what Mr Bainbridge had to say?

Deborah No. I've never had any dealings with this Mr Bainbridge. He's obviously new. I've not been near the firm for years.

Marion He couldn't find our file at first. Then when he did he was mystified. That was his word "mystified". And no wonder really. Here was I asking him to draw up my will, leaving *Curlews* to my sister. And here was he saying I didn't own *Curlews* in the first place. Are you listening?

Deborah Some sort of mistake ——

Marion Mr Bainbridge rifled back through the old documents and what do you think? He said that Dadda's will had specified that you, Deborah, were to inherit the house. That his elder daughter Deborah, was to inherit *Curlews*. There it was in black and white, Deborah. I saw it for myself. For the first time.

Deborah (*desperately*) Marion, there must have been a misunderstanding …!

Marion Was there?

Deborah All those years ago ——

Marion Yes, all those years ago when I was on the other side of the world. When I came home you told me Dadda had left *Curlews* to me. I never doubted your word. Why should I? Why would you say it was mine when it was yours?

Deborah (*floundering*) You've got it all wrong … !

Marion Don't, Deborah. Mr Bainbridge showed me all the letters they wrote and the papers you signed. You knew *Curlews* was yours. Just as Dadda had said.

Deborah Marion — I — you … (*She turns away*)

Marion I thought a lot about why you might have done this, Deborah. I wondered and wondered. I got the clue when Mr Bainbridge said, quite innocently, "Miss Deborah Brown is certainly the owner of *Curlews*. But you have been living in the house too, I gather. And running things for her. Taking care of her." Then I saw it all.

Marion leans accusingly across the table at Deborah

The guilt card! How well you played it!

Deborah (*with spirit*) Has your life been so terrible?

Marion Oh, no! It's just gone on as it did before! Before Dadda died. Before Donald came!

Deborah And went! If he'd been anything of a man he'd have stayed!

Marion No ——

Deborah Or made you go with him!

Marion No — what he did wrong was to give me an impossible choice.

Deborah Well, it amounted to the same thing, didn't it!

Marion (*passionately*) Maybe. But at least he didn't pretend he couldn't live without me! He didn't play the guilt card!

Deborah Perhaps he should have!

Marion No! No. Not such a bad egg.

Marion turns away, controlling her emotion. She puts on her jacket

Deborah (*rising*) Where did you leave the car?

Marion (*brusquely*) Just along.
Deborah Not too far I hope.
Marion Not too far.

Marion starts to fold up the table and finds it heavy

Deborah Leave it! Mr Seagrim will put everything away.
Marion Yes.
Deborah That trip to town has taken it out of you, Marion.
Marion You could say that.
Deborah Now you know how I feel sometimes. (*She moves* R) Stick!

Marion picks up Deborah's walking stick. She stands holding it

  We haven't far to go I hope?
Marion No. There isn't much further to go.
Deborah What? (*She turns back and finds Marion facing her*)

The pair stand in a tense moment of silence

Marion It was a mean trick wasn't it?

Deborah stares defiantly, then at last lowers her eyes

Deborah So. I'm sorry. There.
Marion A bit late.
Deborah Oh don't make a meal of it.
Marion I'll try not to.

Deborah reaches for her stick. Marion holds the stick just out of Deborah's reach. Deborah stumbles as she grasps for the stick

  Didn't you ever worry that I'd find out? Or did you think I was so stupid, that you were safe?
Deborah Don't look at me like that, Marion.
Marion Like what?
Deborah As if you could kill me.
Marion Oh Deborah, you know I wouldn't.
Deborah Of course you wouldn't. What an idea.
Marion It is isn't it? (*She grips the stick like a weapon*)
Deborah Oh do stop it! You'd never hurt a fly.
Marion Then why are you so bothered?
Deborah Because I need my stick.

Marion Just think, I'd have nothing to lose.
Deborah I'm perfectly sure —— !
Marion Oh, but you're not sure, Deborah. How could you be. Not now …
Deborah You're talking like a fool, Marion. Give me my stick.

At last, Marion gives Deborah the stick. Deborah starts to move UR. *Marion picks up her handbag*

You'll feel better when we get to the top of the cliff.
Marion (*quietly*) You may be right. (*She looks upwards towards the clifftop*) Yes, I think I might. We'll see.

Deborah glances back once, uncertainly and then she exits

Marion watches Deborah go; then she follows

Sound of waves

The CURTAIN *falls*

THEATRICAL DIGS

CHARACTERS

Maggie Festoon, an actress; elderly
Pascaline Holbein, an actress; middle-aged

Scene — an esplanade at a seaside resort
Time — the present

The esplanade at a seaside resort. A sunny day

Two beach chairs stand C, facing front

The sound of waves crashing on to the beach

As the CURTAIN *rises, Maggie Festoon is sprawled asleep in one of the chairs. She is an elderly woman, dressed in dark colours and with eccentric, tatty grandeur. She has a pair of spectacles hanging around her neck with a various assortment of scarves and things. Slumped, as she is now, she resembles a dusty pile of charity shop throwouts. On the chair beside her lies her large holdall handbag*

Pascaline Holbein approaches, looking about for a free chair. She is dressed in casual but stylish clothes. She is an actress, middle-aged but looks younger and has about her a studied air of glamour. She too carries a holdall handbag

With an unlovely snore, Maggie's mouth sags open

Pascaline observes the sleeping figure of Maggie. Still, the chair beside Maggie seems to be the only one available. Quietly, Pascaline draws the chair further away from the sleeping Maggie. Pascaline sees Maggie's handbag, picks it up and delicately places it on the ground beside its owner. She settles herself into the chair, takes a small package from her holdall and unwraps it. It is a bun and Pascaline starts to nibble it

Maggie stirs. Without opening her eyes, she feels for the second chair which was beside her, and finds that it has gone. She wakes fully and takes in the situation. Fumbling about, she locates her handbag with a relieved grunt. She stares across at Pascaline

Pascaline nods back and goes on eating daintily

Maggie fumbles around her neck. She finds her spectacles amongst an assortment of things dangling there. She perches them on her nose and looks across at Pascaline. Then she removes the spectacles, cleans them on one of her scarves and replaces them

The sound of waves fades away

Maggie (*again peering at Pascaline*) I seem to know your face, dear.

Pascaline (*charmingly*) Oh, well that is possible.

Maggie (*after a pause*) Seems sort of familiar.

Pascaline It could be.

Maggie Do you do my Meals-on-Wheels?

Pascaline (*less charmingly*) No.

Maggie Oh. (*Pause*) You're not on the Sainsbury's check-out.

Pascaline No I am not.

Maggie No. Still it's familiar. Not a shop. More an office. (*Pause*) Citizens Advice Bureau? (*Pause*) Age Concern?

Pascaline finishes her bun, screws up the wrapper, pops it in her holdall, and turns to face Maggie

Pascaline (*archly*) I might as well confess. You could have seen me on television.

Maggie Could I?

Pascaline Yes, you could. I'm an actress.

Maggie Oh. (*Pause*) *EastEnders*?

Pascaline No.

Maggie No? So what could I have seen you in? *Corona*——

Pascaline No. In a costume series.

Maggie Really. Which one?

Pascaline "The House of Playfairs."

Maggie What? Speak up, dear.

Pascaline "Playfairs."

Maggie I don't remember that.

Pascaline (*kindly*) Well, there are so many popular series on the box.

Maggie How long did it run? Mm?

Pascaline Seven episodes.

Maggie Pardon?

Pascaline Seven episodes.

Maggie Only seven. I see. When was it on then?

Pascaline A little while ago. (*She would like to change the subject. She points seaward*) Oh look … a cormorant, I think.

Maggie About two years ago?

Pascaline Possibly.

Maggie Never saw it. But I remember your face. Very well.

Pascaline (*mollified*) Ah.

Maggie Not from the telly though.

Pascaline Oh.

Maggie More recently. Like today.

Pascaline Well, I am sitting next to you, aren't I?

Maggie No, no. Now don't tell me. You're on a poster advertising something, aren't you. Am I getting warm?

Pascaline Is this Twenty Questions?

Maggie You're not standing for the local council?

Pascaline No, I am not standing for the local council!

Maggie But you're on a poster. I passed it as I came along the front. By the pier. I've got it. You're on that billboard, aren't you?

Pascaline My photograph is on the theatre poster if that's what you mean.

Maggie Theatre poster …

Pascaline On the billing …

Maggie Got it! You're playing on the end of the pier.

Pascaline Yes.

Maggie Well fancy!

Pascaline Yes. At the Pier Theatre.

Maggie I knew I'd seen your face.

Pascaline You've been to see the show then?

Maggie No. On the poster by the pier. You should have said.

Pascaline (*charming again*) I do apologize. But one does get stopped so often, for autographs and all that. I just slipped out before the matinée for a breath of fresh air. Usually I stay in my dressing room and a stage-hand runs out for a sandwich for me. I need to rest a bit, you understand. It's quite demanding. My voice ——

Maggie Singer are you? "Starlight Follies"?

Pascaline No, that's on the other pier ——

Maggie I always like musical shows. But that's right, they're mostly on the other pier. On this pier it's usually Sooty or Postman Pat or ——

Pascaline I do sing, of course. And dance. One needs to be prepared for anything in the profession. But it's a straight play this time — a serious drama.

Maggie (*surprised*) Oh the pier?

Pascaline Yes! It's called *Black Chiffon*.

Maggie *Black Chiffon*. That takes me back.

Pascaline You know the play?

Maggie Just about.

Pascaline It's a revival.

Maggie That's a change.

Pascaline It's a pre-London try-out.

Maggie On the pier?

Pascaline Yes! After here we go on tour. And then we'll go into the West End, in London.

Maggie Oh. Nice. What part are you taking then?

Pascaline The lead. The major role.

Maggie Ooh. Good gracious.

*Pascaline shoots Maggie a tiny suspicious glance. But Maggie appears to be
agog with interest*

Pascaline Yes. A star part, of course. She's a woman who is at a crisis in her
life. Age-wise. Feeling the middle years creeping up on her. Her children
flying the nest. She's worried about her husband. Worried about her figure.
Worried about her lines.

Maggie Doesn't she know them?

Pascaline On her face! On her face! So she takes to shop-lifting. And she
steals this glamorous négligé. It's a statement, of course.

Maggie Of course.

Pascaline It's a heartcry. Every woman will sympathize with her tangled
emotions. She's in menopausal turmoil. Irrational decisions, uncharacter-
istic actions, mental aberrations, erratic behaviour patterns ——

Maggie Doesn't she get arrested?

Pascaline Yes. It brings everything to a head.

Maggie Well it would.

Pascaline It's a very demanding part. Do you get the local paper?

Maggie I get the freebie.

Pascaline Did you see our review?

Maggie Was it the one that said "The prompt rapidly established herself as
a firm favourite with the audience" ?

Pascaline No, it was not.

Maggie I was pulling your leg, dear.

Pascaline It was a very good notice — particularly for me.

Maggie Congratulations.

Pascaline Would you like me to arrange a complimentary ticket for you?

Maggie That is kind of you, dear. But it's not necessary ——

Pascaline I'm sure you'd enjoy it. There's another matinée on Saturday, if
you don't want to be out late at night.

Maggie No, that's not it ——

Pascaline Don't you like the theatre?

Maggie I love it, dear ——

Pascaline (*grandly*) Then why won't you let me arrange a complimentary
ticket for you?

Maggie Because I can get one any time.

Pascaline Oh. (*Less grandly*) Well, I know the houses aren't exactly packed
out but ——

Maggie No, I mean, I know Bernie on the stage door and he'll always fix me
up.

Pascaline Oh, I see. How nice. So you'll come.

Maggie I'll try, dear. I may not be free ——

Pascaline Well, let's hope there's a little slot in your social diary, shall we?

Maggie Oh I'm not gadding about, dear. I'm waiting for some news and it might change my circumstances a bit, so I'm sort of on call.

Pascaline I see. As a matter of fact I'm waiting on a call too. From my agent. There's the possibility of a film with — well you wouldn't know his name, but he's very big in Hollywood. I've done lots of film work, of course, but I told my agent "You simply have to contact that director for me — he's casting this major film in London right now ——"

Maggie I wish you luck, dear.

Pascaline Thank you so much. If you'd like my autograph ——

Maggie I haven't got a pen handy.

Pascaline When you come to the theatre perhaps.

Maggie Thank you, dear. What was your name again?

Pascaline Pascaline Holbein.

Maggie Who thought that up then?

Pascaline It happens to be my real name. We don't change them nowadays — unless there is another actor with the same name.

Maggie Well you were safe there, I suppose. How long have you been in the business, dear?

Pascaline Oh, some years. First, I went to RADA when I was about eighteen. That's the Royal Academy of Dramatic Art, you know.

Maggie Ah.

Pascaline Yes.

Maggie It's not so easy to get in these days, I believe.

Pascaline (*shooting Maggie a look*) Then I went into the West End.

Maggie That was quick wasn't it?

Pascaline As the juvenile lead. That doesn't mean I was a juvenile. It's just a theatrical term.

Maggie I know.

Pascaline Then afterwards there was TV and radio and I went on tours, major productions, all over the world and ... What did you say?

Maggie When?

Pascaline Why did you say "I know" in that way.

Maggie How do you mean, dear?

Pascaline Meaningly.

Maggie Did I?

Pascaline It occurs to me that you're familiar with the language of the theatre.

Maggie You could say that. yes.

Pascaline Oh, I see. Well, you should have mentioned your interest. Though I should have guessed when you said you knew the stage-door keeper at the Pier. Aren't you naughty! Amdram, are we? Not nowadays I suppose. Drama teacher sometime were we, in a local school?

Maggie Oh no, dear.

Pascaline Don't tell me you were an actress like me.

Maggie Well I've never seen you act, dear.

Pascaline You're teasing me now. You were in the profession too! How lovely! Tell me your name.

Maggie Maggie Festoon.

Pascaline Maggie Festoon! It rings a bell. So you retired down here to the seaside. Such a nice place.

Maggie Lovely dear. And we get some wonderful companies playing here.

Pascaline (*smugly*) Yes, of course.

Maggie In the town. At the Royalty.

Pascaline (*crossly*) Yes, of course. It's a touring date.

Maggie I thought you were on tour. Pre-London ——

Pascaline That's right!

Maggie Well you certainly never know in this business. Anything can happen.

Pascaline gives Maggie a hard stare. Then goes into the attack herself

Pascaline Would you have played in anything special? Anything I'd remember?

Maggie Juliet's nurse, dear. Perhaps. At Stratford.

Pascaline Stratford E?

Maggie On Avon.

Pascaline Fancy. Some while back, mm?

Maggie A notable season, dear. Believe me, I've played with all the greats. Yes. Sods to a man.

Pascaline Oh!

Maggie I'm kidding dear! Don't take it so seriously.

Pascaline I'm sorry, but I take the profession very seriously indeed. As most actors do — these days.

Maggie Oh I agree, dear. Flog yourselves silly. And that's just at the read-through.

Pascaline We like to explore a character in depth — peel away the outer layers, like skins of an onion ——

Maggie You're making me cry already. Have you ever peeled away the skins of an onion, dear? In the end there's nothing.

Pascaline Some of us like to discover some essential facet of our own being as we develop a character. I just love to work with thrusting new young directors with probing intellects — who like to experiment with the textual patterns — workshopping — improvising — discovering ——

Maggie Yes, well... playing in weekly rep twice-nightly, we didn't go in for a lot of that. You know I could run my hand down a page of dialogue and I'd know it spot on.

Pascaline I don't imagine those old plays were difficult to learn.

Maggie That's true. Well written, I suppose. Yes, rehearsed in the morning, played at five and eight — and three times on Wednesday and Saturdays — washed our hair and sorted out our frocks on Sunday — and still had time for a colourful sex-life.

Pascaline It must have all been very superficial.

Maggie Deeply, dear.

Pascaline I mean what about the sub-text?

Maggie Sub-text?

Pascaline The hidden meaning.

Maggie Oh, that struggled up about Thursday.

Pascaline Well I prefer time to discuss my character with the rest of the cast, get the mood right — and the atmosphere — get to grips with my true feelings. I like to learn something about myself as a person when I work on a part. Getting down to the basic truth, the reality within the art form ——

Maggie Well, just so long as you can make yourself heard, dear. Out there on the pier — with the waves crashing about under you.

Pascaline Of course I can!

Maggie Mind you, I'll grant it's easier today — television and film — little bits of scenes and stacks more money. And commercials. Have you done commercials?

Pascaline Well yes. I've done commercials.

Maggie I love making commercials. They all know their job on commercials. Real professionals. Only once ever had a bad time on a commercial. That was when I worked with a chimpanzee.

Pascaline A chimpanzee?

Maggie Called Charlie he was. I think the product was some sort of teabag.

Pascaline Seems likely.

Maggie He wasn't trained properly, that was the trouble. The wretched animal ran riot, upset the teapot, threw sugar lumps at me, snatched off my wig. The crew were in fits — until he started swinging on the cables. Blue sparks flying everywhere. Horrible little beast. But I fixed him.

Pascaline Whatever did you do?

Maggie I spiked his banana.

Pascaline Pardon?

Maggie His morning snack.

Pascaline Oh.

Maggie Yes. He ran up the scenery, turned three somersaults and fell down dead. Well good as.

Pascaline Some spike. What was in it?

Maggie I never reveal my professional secrets, dear. But be advised, never work with a chimpanzee. Even if it's a Tarzan film.

Pascaline I don't think they make Tarzan films any more.

Maggie They will, take my word.

Pascaline But they'll use animatronics, I expect, like in *Jurassic Park*.

Maggie I sincerely hope so. Those chimpanzees are always showing up somewhere. What an agent they've got!

Pascaline I haven't done too many commercials. One doesn't want one's face to get too familiar on the screen or one isn't used for real parts. I mean you can't be advertising dandruff shampoo one night and taking a serious dramatic role the next.

Maggie I don't know. I think you're splitting hairs. Ha ha! But it's certainly where the money is, television — I should have made a fortune ——

Pascaline But there's nothing like a live audience, when you can hear a pin drop, or there's a great gale of laughter!

Maggie Always providing it's a comedy, of course.

Pascaline laughs in spite of herself

Pascaline I'm sure you miss the life, don't you? Deep down.

Maggie Well, no, because ——

Pascaline Now don't deny it. Not to me. I understand. I can't imagine never talking shop with other actors. Never discussing the reviews with friends in the theatre ——

Maggie No, you don't understand ——

Pascaline But it must! You must miss the company. Have you never thought of applying to go into Denville Hall? You'd love it!

Maggie Denville Hall?

Pascaline The home for old actors! Think of it!

Maggie I am.

Pascaline I could use my influence to get you in, I'm sure. I mean even if your Equity card has run out ——

Maggie It hasn't.

Pascaline I'd be happy to vouch for you. I'm sure you're just the type of person. You'd be the life and soul ... And if you're likely to be moving anyway. What was it you said? Changed circumstances? Waiting on a sheltered flat, are we?

Maggie No, I'm not waiting on a sheltered flat ——

Pascaline Look, I'm going to phone my agent. Not another word! She knows all about these things. She's on the management committee or something, I believe. She's always selling me raffle tickets anyway. (*She takes out a mobile phone from her holdall, and stabs a couple of digits into it*)

Maggie It's really not necessary ——

Pascaline Now don't give it another thought. As a matter of fact I wanted to ring her anyway. One likes to keep in touch, you know. (*Into phone*) Helen! How are you? ... Oh hallo, Janey. It's Pascaline here. Is Helen there?... Pascaline Holbein ... In a meeting? Ah. ... What? ... Pascaline. Pascaline Holbein ... You know, down at ... Yes ... *Black Chiffon* ... Oh yes marvellous, darling ... They're rivetted ... Packing out ... What?... Oh. Did Helen speak to ... Yes. ... Oh. Well when? When is he coming over? I thought he was coming this week. .... Oh, he's gone back. Are you sure?... I see. Are you sure Helen's not there, I thought I heard her cough. Ha ha, no mistaking it!... I see. Right. Be in touch.(*She folds the phone away and replaces it in her bag. She then becomes aware of Maggie and remembers what she was supposed to be making the call for*) So sorry. It wasn't the moment.

Maggie I'm trying to tell you, dear, I'm not interested in Denville Hall.

Pascaline But it's beautiful. The grounds. The house. The food. And I believe they even have an amateur dramatic society and everything. Lots of big stars visit regularly. I know I'd just love to live there.

Maggie Then why don't you?

Pascaline I shall certainly put my name down in due course. When I'm nearer the age. Thirty years' time or so. I believe there's a huge waiting list.

Maggie Listen dear, I'm sure your heart's in the right place ... Isn't that a funny saying? If your heart wasn't in the right place you'd probably be seriously ill. Ha ha! No, as I say, I'm sure you mean well but the point is ——

There is the sound of a mobile phone bleeping. Pascaline at once dives for her bag and fumbles in it, looking for her mobile phone

Pascaline Excuse me a moment, I expect it's my agent calling back. (*She finds her phone and answers it*) Hallo? Hallo? Pascaline Holbein here!

The mobile continues bleeping. Maggie searches about her own person and at last locates her own mobile from the depths of her clothing. The bleep stops as Maggie answers the telephone. Pascaline stares at Maggie

Maggie (*into the phone*) Hallo? Oh hallo, Barry. .... No, no problem, I'm just sitting here in the sun chatting to a friend. I thought you might call. ... Yes. Go on. (*Hissing across at Pascaline*) Sorry. It's my agent.

Pascaline Agent?

Maggie (*into the phone*) Yes. ... Really! Oh yes, that would be nice. So you've put me up have you? ... Oh, thank you, dear. Mm. Who's doing the screenplay? ... Ooo! He's so good at the biographical stuff. ... A long one. ... I should think so, she had a long life.

Pascaline (*eagerly*) Whose life? Who?
Maggie (*into the phone*) A wonderful subject. Which company?
Pascaline Which company? BBC?
Maggie (*into the phone*) Oh, they can afford all those locations ...
Pascaline Who can? Which locations?
Maggie (*into the phone*) When are they casting? Yes ... yes ...
Pascaline Who's casting? Where? When?

Pascaline stabs a number into her own phone

Maggie (*still on her own phone*) What dear? ... Wait a moment I'll write it
down. Just find a pencil ... And a bit of paper ... Oh dear. ... Barry, two
minutes, darling. (*She puts down phone*) Pencil — paper ...

*Maggie starts another search of her belongings. Pascaline is now through
to her agent*

Pascaline (*into the phone*) Helen?... Ah caught you. Listen I've just heard
there a major production being set up — and the main role sounds like
something for me. It's a sort of biography of some terribly famous woman
or other ... What? Who?... Yes, that'll be it. You knew! Why didn't you
call me? Well, just tell me all about it now! Yes. ... Yes. ... Look, hold, on
I want to write it down. ... Just finding a pen and paper. ... I know I have
a pen here somewhere. ... (*She puts down her phone and rummages
around, emptying out the contents of her bag. Her diary is amongst the
items*)

*The two mobile phones get moved around from place to place as the two
women search for pen and paper, and in the process get mixed up*

*Maggie finds a pencil. She spots the diary which has fallen out of Pascaline's
bag. Maggie grabs it*

  (*Grabbing the diary back*) Do you mind!
Maggie Can I just have a page?
Pascaline That's my diary!
Maggie The blank bit at the end? I'll lend you my pencil.
Pascaline Oh all right! (*She tears out a page of her diary and takes Maggie's
pencil*)

*Meantime, Maggie spots Pascaline's pen and picks it up. They find the
phones. Each has the phone belonging to the other. Both women poise
themselves to write. Pascaline scratches at the paper*

  (*With a cry of rage*)This point's broken!

Maggie Is it?

Pascaline And that's my pen you've got there!

Maggie Is it? It was just lying around.

Pascaline Give it here! (*She grabs the pen back*)

Maggie You know I've just remembered ... (*She feels in a pocket and brings out a neat notepad, with a biro attached*)

Pascaline (*looking at the phone in her hand*) And now Helen's cut off! Honestly!

The phone in Pascaline's hand suddenly bleeps

Oh, no she hasn't. (*Into the phone*) Hallo?... Yes I'm still here. ... Yes. ... Yes. ... (*Writing*) Yes, I've got that. ...(*Pleased*) Oh good. ... Well, thank you. ... (*Her smile turns to puzzlement*) You told them what? That's stretching it a bit isn't it? ... (*Chuckling*) But, well, if you think ... What? ... Hold on, who is that?... Barry who?... Isn't that Helen? You sound like Helen. ... Are you sure?... All right, all right.... No I'm not! Just a minute!... Hold on. ... I said hold on! (*She holds out the phone to Maggie*) It's for you!

Maggie stares at the phone in her own hand. Pascaline snatches her own phone from Maggie. She slaps the other phone on to Maggie's lap. Pascaline thumps at the digits on her own phone. The following telephone conversations happen more or less simultaneously. Both women write busily as they listen and take notes

Maggie (*into her own phone*) Hallo? Barry?... Yes, it's me now. Bit of a mix-up. Sorry darling. Now then let's have the details. ... Mm. ... Yes. ... Mm. ... Yes. ... Mm. ... Mm. ... Fine. Thank you, dear. ... that's very sweet of you. I've not played many saints. I wonder why? You don't have to answer that. I must say it sounds very jolly. ... But never count our chicks, eh? Let me know what they say. ... You will. ... Today. ... Oh good.

Pascaline (*into her own phone*) So can I have the details. ... Mm. ... Mm. ... Yes. ... Mm ... Yes ... What?... Yes. ... Mm. ... Right. About the part, Helen. It is Helen? ... Never mind. ... It does sound so right for me, don't you think? ... What? Well, it depends how they see that character, doesn't it?... That's what acting is about, Helen. ... Will you speak to them right away?... They can see my picture in *Spotlight* ... What? ... Well if you think it best. ... I ... Oh ... (*The phone has gone dead*)

The two women fold up their phones and put them aside

Pascaline My agent is ringing the producer right away. She thinks I'm absolutely right for the part.

Maggie Really. I'd have thought you were a bit glam, dear. I suppose you could wear a tatty grey wig.

Pascaline She didn't have hair anyway. She always wore a scarf.

Maggie She must have had hair sometime.

Pascaline It was a distinctive sort of biblical headress. Very characteristic. Very individual.

Maggie Like Yasser Arafat. Same milliner, I'm told.

Pascaline Oh do shut up. It's a star role. I wonder why Helen didn't tell me. You may be right about my age. She still sees me as an *ingénue* sometimes. Silly woman.

Maggie Silly woman.

Pascaline I hope she remembers to mention I spent a lot of my girlhood in India.

Maggie What as?

Pascaline What do you mean "what as". I was a child. I had an Ayah and everything. Come to think of it she looked like her. She was so sweet.

Maggie Maybe it *was* her. Were you rescued from a gutter in Calcutta?

Pascaline No I was not rescued from a gutter in Calcutta!

Maggie Sounds like a cue for song. Now if they make the musical ——

Pascaline You are impossible! Can't you even be serious at this moment?

Maggie Listen, if I was serious at this moment, I'd be very annoyed at you ringing your agent and trying to get my part. And if I thought you stood a chance of getting it, I'd be very seriously put out. As it is ——

Pascaline As it is you think you'll get it. Well, I know how these producers work. They'll never cast an old actress in a role like this. I mean think, it'll probably be a year before they start shooting then a couple of years in the making. How do you know you won't turn up your toes? I don't mean to sound unkind but you might not stay the pace.

Maggie Well she did.

Pascaline Anyway, it's all in the playing. I understand the background of the woman.

Maggie And all they'll have to do is cover your face with rubber wrinkles, put black contacts in your eyes, knock out a tooth or two … and saw you off at the knees.

Pascaline Don't be ridiculous.

Maggie Well let's face it, saint she might have been; but she was skinny as a bird, with a little round head and brown wizened skin and ——

The two mobile phones both begin to bleep. Both women dive to answer them

Pascaline (*into the phone*) Helen?
Maggie (*into the phone*) Barry?

Both woman listen attentively, making only little murmurs in response. The
hopeful light on each face slowly dies out

(*At last, into the phone*) Thanks Barry. (*She folds away her mobile*)
Pascaline (*into the phone*) Thanks Helen. (*She folds away her mobile*)
Maggie (*to Pascaline*) Mm?
Pascaline (*shaking her head and looking enquiringly*) Mm?

Maggie shakes her head. The two women shrug. Then in concert , let out a
furious and noisy howl. They recover themselves

Maggie Who cares.
Pascaline Who cares.

They both turn to each other and weep loudly and mockingly on each other's
shoulders. They dry up

Maggie
Pascaline } (*together*) Oh well.
Pascaline Producer said I was too old.
Maggie The producer thinks I'm too young.
Pascaline Apparently they want a genuine ethnic type. And all skin and bone
   with a face like a wizened walnut, coal black eyes and no teeth.
Maggie Yes. And it's cast already.
Pascaline Oh! Who got it?
Maggie Three guesses.
Pascaline What? But she's fair and cuddly with blue eye and dimples ——
Maggie But short. They won't need to cut her off at the knees.
Pascaline No,
Maggie If she weren't such a love, she'd be seriously unpopular.
Pascaline Yes.

Maggie rummages about in her pockets and brings out a bag of sweets

Maggie (*offering the bag*) Jelly baby?
Pascaline Thanks. (*She takes a sweet and puts it in her mouth*)
Maggie What time did you say your matinée was?
Pascaline (*spitting out the sweet*) Oh God, it's gone the half! And I've got
   to run the length of the pier!
Maggie You'll never make it — being so old!

The two women collect up their belongings

No problem, of course, for a spring chicken like me!

Pascaline You're coming to the matinée?
Maggie Wouldn't miss it.
Pascaline Thanks!
Maggie I know somebody in the cast.
Pascaline Oh? Who?
Maggie You.

Pascaline starts out

  A sensational actress, I understand.
Pascaline (*returning*) Oh. Really? (*Pleased*) Who said so?
Maggie It's on your billing.
Pascaline (*crossly*) Bitch! (*She starts out, then stops and turns back. She
  smiles at Maggie ruefully*) I apologize.
Maggie Don't mention it. We bitches must stick together. And it's twenty
  to three.

  Pascaline gives a shriek of panic and dashes off

See you later, Pascaline Holbein!

Maggie makes a stately exit following after Pascaline

(*Singing*) She was found in a gutter in Calcutta … Calcutta in a gutter. She
was called little Ransid Yakbutta … In Calcutta …

The CURTAIN *falls*

SHORT CHANGED

CHARACTERS

Miss Westlake, a retired headmistress; eighties
Julia Griffith, social service official; about fifty

Scene — the gardens of *Merrywinds*, a residential
home overlooking the sea
Time — the present

The gardens of Merrywinds, *a residential home, overlooking the sea. A sunny day*

Three top-range canvas chairs are set casually DS, *facing front. Miss Westlake is seated in the centre chair. Another chair is set further to the* R

Miss Westlake sits taking in the atmosphere and sniffing approvingly. She is a retired headmistress in her eighties and she retains a manner of authority. She wears a smart, if unfashionable suit, and nearby she has a large handbag

Julia Griffith, a social services official, aged about fifty, enters UR. *She is an attractive, pleasant woman with a brisk, but not officious manner. She carries a clipboard and a folder. She has a mobile phone attached to her and has a rose tucked into her pocket. She spots Miss Westlake and comes down to her* R, *with a friendly smile*

Julia Ah ha, there you are. They told me you were up in the Rose Garden.
Miss Westlake Did they?
Julia They did, they did.
Miss Westlake I preferred to sit here.
Julia Never mind. It wasn't a wasted journey. The scent was wonderful. (*Casually offering the rose*) Would you like this? (*Pause*) I didn't pick it, it had fallen off.

Miss Westlake gives no response

Julia tosses the rose into the furthest chair R. *She then sits down next to Miss Westlake*

Miss Westlake I like the sea air.
Julia (*tidying the folder*) A bit bracing sometimes. Better for kites. Just let me get these papers firmly under control. (*Jokily*) You wouldn't be very pleased with me if Mrs Fanshawe's personal particulars floated off on a sudden eddy. And got washed up all along the beach. Would you? Who would!
Miss Westlake I beg your pardon?
Julia It has happened. Mercifully, the water had washed off the details! (*She pauses, expecting a reaction*)

Miss Westlake gives no response

A long time ago, of course. And only once. Personally, I think it's just a story. (*She settles to business*) Now then. Mrs Ellen Fanshawe, isn't it ?

Miss Westlake Who is?

Julia You is. I mean — wait a moment. (*She flicks through the papers*) Right.
You are Mrs Ellen Fanshawe——

Miss Westlake No, I am not.

Julia But this is Mrs Ellen Fanshawe's file. The one I have here. Um. You've
no connection … ?

Miss Westlake Not at all.

Julia Sheesh. What have they given me?

Miss Westlake The wrong file apparently.

Julia So it would seem. We do get a great many applications for *Merrywinds
House*, Mrs ——

Miss Westlake Miss.

Julia Miss Fan ——

Miss Westlake Westlake.

Julia Westlake?

Miss Westlake E. M.

Julia Well, we have one initial correct. It's a start.

Miss Westlake The E does not stand for Ellen.

Julia (*studying the papers*) And I don't suppose you have two daughters in
Australia? No. Nor are you a war widow, I'll hazard a guess. Oh dear. Yes,
I'm afraid it is certainly the wrong file. (*She smiles at Miss Westlake*) We'll
sort it out.

Miss Westlake I hope so.

Julia Excuse me. (*She rises and moves DR. She takes her mobile phone, stabs
out a number and waits; into the phone*) Jill? I have the wrong papers here.
I need Miss Westlake's file. It's a new application. …Yes. …Yes. … Yes
Jill. … Yes, I know. But could you find the file and send Bobbie down with
it? We're on the cliff seats. Miss E. M. Westlake. You gave me Mrs Ellen
Fanshawe. … What? All right, I *took* Mrs Ellen Fanshawe. It's Westlake
I'm after right now. … Yes, all right. Just find it and send it down, will you?
I can have a talk with Miss —Westlake, meantime. She's been sitting here
for ——

Miss Westlake Half an hour.

Julia Half an hour. Thank you, Jill. … Yes, thank you. Thank you. (*She puts
away the phone*) I'm so sorry about that, Miss Westlake. It isn't usual. The
office is very efficient. Known for it. In fact, the whole of the staff at
Merrywinds are thoroughly reliable. It's one of the best of the residential
homes we administer. (*She crosses L above Miss Westlake, indicating the
house in the distance*)

Miss Westlake I'm aware of that.

Julia In fact, it's one of the reasons we can accept so few of the applications.
I wish we had more *Merrywinds*. But it's very special. The house itself is
so elegant — the best sort of early Victorian — and the position here
overlooking the sea …

Miss Westlake Quite. That is why I chose it.

Julia Ah. Yes. Well, I know it's your preference ——

Miss Westlake It is where I wish to live. To spend my remaining years.

Julia Of course. (*She moves down to the chair, L of Miss Westlake. Sitting*) The problem is, Miss Westlake, that *Merrywinds* always has a waiting list ——

Miss Westlake I am aware of that also. That was why I made this appointment. I was informed that I should be recommended for the first vacancy that occurs. In view of the circumstances.

Julia Circumstances? (*She opens the folder; then remembers and closes it with a slap*) Tch! Silly me. Would you like to tell me a little more … ? I am so sorry I haven't the full picture right this minute.

Miss Westlake You are the right person to refer to?

Julia Yes, insofar as ——

Miss Westlake I have been through the assessment process. Before the Board. Henry Redfern is the Chairman. It was quite satisfactory.

Julia That's good.

Miss Westlake It was implied that the final analysis was up to you, Miss … er … Griffiths. And you would find me an acceptable suite. Just as soon as one became available. That is your function, isn't it?

Julia It is my responsibility …

Miss Westlake When you do get access to my papers you will see my background. No doubt you will be reassured that I will make a suitable resident.

A pause

Julia You know, Miss Westlake, *Merrywinds* was established by a rather unusual Trust Fund. It means it can be run more like a five-star hotel than a residential home. So I am sure you appreciate that there is a great demand ——

Miss Westlake I do understand that.

Julia In consequence, it is sometimes quite difficult to ——

Miss Westlake In my lifelong career I had similar pressures. To make choices. To make decisions ——

Julia's mobile phone bleeps

Julia Excuse me a moment. (*Answering the phone*) Yes? … Oh, what a nuisance. … Well as soon as you can, please. … No, it's not exactly urgent. … Right. … Yes. … Exactly. We'll get to know each other. (*She replaces the phone and smiles at Miss Westlake*) After all, that is what this meeting is all about. It just would have helped if … Oh well. Where were we? So —what was your lifelong career, Miss Westlake?

Miss Westlake I was headmistress of a boarding school. A school with a very exceptional academic record.

Julia A headmistress ——

Miss Westlake Of a girls' school. There was a school for girls along the coast here, called *Deacons* ——

Julia *Deacons*?

Miss Westlake You knew it? Oh, you're local then.

Julia No. But I knew it. (*Her manner changes from now on. It becomes less light and more wry*)

Miss Westlake (*without noticing Julia's change of manner*) It was a fine school. But it is no longer in existence, I'm afraid. I believe it's a hotel nowadays.

Julia It isn't a school any more.

Miss Westlake *Deacons* was a private educational establishment. We had the daughters of diplomats, consuls and some very high-ranking army officers. And a few lesser personnel and government officials serving overseas. Just a few, you understand. Not many.

Julia Just a sprinkling.

Miss Westlake You might put it that way. Anyhow all the girls were from good families and our reputation such that we could pick and choose our pupils. Yes, the entrance examination for *Deacons* was one of the most stringent in the country, they told me. Did you go to a school with high academic standards. Miss ... er —— ?

Julia Yes, I went to a school with high academic standards.

Miss Westlake Then you know how important these things are.

Julia Yes, I do.

Miss Westlake You went to university?

Julia No, I didn't.

Miss Westlake What a pity.

Julia I thought so at one time. Not now.

Miss Westlake These days standards are falling everywhere. At *Deacons* there was a pass rate of ninety-five percent. By the time I retired our success was a phenomenon. It was all due to our policy of selection.

Julia Selection?

Miss Westlake We employed only the highest qualified teaching staff and we admitted only the brightest pupils. That was the secret of our success.

Julia You could hardly fail.

Miss Westlake On the contrary. The young do not always develop as you expect. They do not always fulfil their early promise. They change. Puberty does odd things to girls.

Julia To boys as well, surely.

Miss Westlake I am speaking about girls. They can get too aware of their bodies. Make unsuitable relationships. They can tail off.

Julia Ah. "Tail off." I'm sure you couldn't allow that.

Miss Westlake Quite. We had an intensive cramming programme. To ensure they got back into the top stream. To make certain they didn't lose sight of their goal.

Julia And spoil your record.

Miss Westlake My aim was always to benefit my girls. Their intellectual development was paramount. But we needed to get results, you understand. And we did.

Julia With all of them?

Miss Westlake There was no "all", there were very few backsliders.

Julia But with the odd failures … ?

Miss Westlake Naturally, we were obliged to weed them out.

Julia "Weed" them out. That sounds like Parazone in the porridge.

Miss Westlake I used a metaphor.

Julia Was that effective? I'm sorry I'm being flippant.

Miss Westlake And I am being serious. I was proud to have been head of *Deacons* for thirty years. I considered it the achievement of my life's ambition.

Julia What exactly happened to *Deacons*?

Miss Westlake I thought you said you were a local person.

Julia No. I said I lived locally for several years. For the last twenty I was living in Cumbria.

Miss Westlake So what are you doing here now. In this sort of position?

Julia It was my latest promotion.

Miss Westlake I see. Interesting to come back to the area.

Julia For you too, I imagine. Why did *Deacons* close?

Miss Westlake It was absorbed into the general education system.

Julia Ah.

Miss Westlake After I retired there were changes …

Julia For the worse or for the better?

Miss Westlake I'm not sure where this conversation is leading, Miss Griffiths. I have told you all I feel is relevant. Yet I detect that you seem to have a rather exceptional interest in *Deacons*. Is there a particular reason for this?

Julia There is, actually.

Miss Westlake I thought there was something. Does it have any bearing on my application to move into *Merrywinds*, may I ask? I have told you my reputation in the world of scholarship ——

Julia It concerns a pupil. A girl ——

Miss Westlake One of my girls? There were so many ——

Julia And you probably won't remember her.

Miss Westlake I certainly won't if you don't tell me her name.

Julia Farthing.

A pause

Miss Westlake Farthing?

Julia She was the daughter of an army man. Her mother died. She was an only child. Later her father was killed in an accident. On an exercise ——

Miss Westlake There's no need to go on. I think I know who you are talking about.

Julia Her school fees continued to be paid by the army ——

Miss Westlake I've told you. I remember her.

Julia I suppose you would describe her as one of the girls who tailed off. Would you?

Miss Westlake What is your particular interest? It's a long time ago.

Julia Would you?

Miss Westlake She was a disappointment certainly.

Julia Yes?

Miss Westlake She was obliged to leave *Deacons* ——

Julia Rather suddenly, I believe. Just before her final exams were coming up. Isn't that right?

Miss Westlake We felt it best. She was no longer suitable to be educated in our establishment. But may I ask … ?

Julia Didn't it make the newspapers?

Miss Westlake Certainly not. Well — some brief reference in the local weekly. Inaccurate, ungrammatical and misspelt.

Julia I knew some of the girls from *Deacons* and they told me part of the story and I wondered about it. They used to call her Penny. Penny Farthing, a schoolgirl nickname ——

Miss Westlake Does this have any bearing on the matter in hand? *Merrywinds*?

Julia I think perhaps it does. The idea is for us to get to know each other. For me to discover the sort of person you are, if you'll forgive me. If you'll — fit in — at *Merrywinds* . I believe the Farthing affair caused quite a stir locally? And you are coming back to your old stamping ground, after all.

Miss Westlake I don't follow your reasoning, Miss — er ... The girl simply couldn't keep up. There was no point in her taking her finals.

Julia But why did she suddenly fall off like that?

Miss Westlake As I said, girls sometimes change direction. Find other things more absorbing in their lives. Running after boys —getting silly ideas about their careers — wanting to be models — or pop stars — that sort of nonsense.

Julia And that's what happened?

Miss Westlake Something like that. She was not university material.

Julia So she didn't want to go.

Miss Westlake It isn't a case of what a girl wants. Her grades have to be maintained. It was quite obvious she was not working. Getting distracted by whims and fancies as some girls do at that age. Not many of mine, fortunately. It was a difficult decision, but we all agreed.

Julia All?

Miss Westlake Other members of the teaching staff. Her English mistress. Her maths. Her housemistress …

Julia Oh yes. (*Carefully*) That was a Miss Bathgate, wasn't it?

Miss Westlake Not Bathgate. Northgate. Betty— (*She corrects herself*) Elizabeth Northgate. She was her housemistress.

Julia You were all of one mind about her, you say.

Miss Westlake Completely.

Julia Even Miss Northgate?

Miss Westlake Excuse me — the sun … (*She brings out a handkerchief and dabs at her brow*)

Julia (*rising*) Too strong? Shall I get an umbrella? (*She moves across the front of the stage to the R*) On second thoughts I think it's too breezy ——

Miss Westlake No matter. No matter.

Julia dumps her folder and clipboard on the far chair R. She perches on the chair's arm and watches Miss Westlake. She waits for a reply

(*Eventually*) I don't know what you heard, but I must admit Miss Northgate was not so convinced as I was. She was such a soft-hearted young woman. Easily won over by a pair of tearful eyes … A girl had only to run to Elizabeth Northgate and tell her some fanciful tale and she would believe every word. But, even she saw in the end that the Farthing girl had to go.

Julia You say "in the end". You mean it took some persuasion to make her decide? And, I suppose, some courage on her part to go against the majority. (*Pause*) Was she afraid of you?

Miss Westlake Afraid! Heavens, that was the last thing — of course not. It was just that the girl had somehow wheedled her way into Elizabeth's affections.

Julia She was her favourite?

Miss Westlake I'm afraid it was so. Always a bad thing, you understand. Clouds the judgement. I saw it coming. I should have done something earlier. Elizabeth behaved very foolishly. Allowed herself to believe the Farthing girl possessed far more ability than she actually did. Constantly giving her extra tutorials. Special coaching. She was never out of Elizabeth's study. She said the girl had great potential. Great potential she might have had but it was not in the brain department.

Julia But it seems to me it was a bit hard to throw the girl out so near to her final exams?

Miss Westlake She would not have passed. As I explained to everyone. Her marks in the mock exams were clear proof even to her housemistress.

Julia But wasn't that odd? Are you certain there was no mistake about those marks? I mean when your teaching standards were so high. There was no other factor? Was the girl sick? Hay fever— a menstrual problem …?

Miss Westlake Not at all —

Julia The loss of her father?

Miss Westlake No, no, no. I'm sure she was over that. And these girls with parents overseas — they don't have very close bonds with them. That is why a teacher must beware of becoming some sort of a substitute. Bad for both of them in the end. You do see that?

Julia I see that.

Miss Westlake Poor Elizabeth; she was quite bewildered by those marks. Found them hard to believe. But there they were. Quite unacceptable, as she had to admit. But it was a blow for her and she needed much consoling. I told her, it was a lesson she had to learn. Not to expect too much of these young things. Not to make favourites. So hurtful when they let you down. They can be so cruel, the young. Often unknowingly.

Julia (*rising and turning away*) Not only the young. And sometimes knowingly.

Miss Westlake What did you say? I didn't quite catch … You do realize, the school's reputation was at stake.

Julia (*turning back*) Just because of that one pupil? You make it sound very fragile.

Miss Westlake You are purposely misunderstanding. You don't appreciate the situation. How can you? There were other aspects. Other considerations.

Julia (*sitting down in the chair* R *of Miss Westlake*) Ah yes. Those other considerations. There were rumours, I believe ——

Miss Westlake Rumours?

Julia I suppose if Miss Northgate "favouring" the girl had been misinterpreted then her reputation might have suffered. And by implication then so might your own … A hint of scandal … I do understand …

Miss Westlake (*firmly*) There was never scandal of any sort connected with *Deacons*. Never! Rumours are the product of idle minds. Of ignorance and envy. As long as they are not fed with titbits of distorted fact they die of starvation.

Julia An innocent schoolgirl crush, perhaps.

A pause

Miss Westlake remains silent

But a serious jolt to the girl's career prospects.

Miss Westlake There were other options. There always are.

Julia So she finished her education elsewhere? How did she do?

Miss Westlake No, no. I don't mean that. I'm sure she didn't go on to great heights, if that's what you think. Despite Elizabeth's remarkable faith in her.

Julia I hope she didn't hold it against you.

Miss Westlake Who?

Julia Penny Farthing, of course.

Miss Westlake Oh, I thought you meant ——

Julia But I do appreciate your position Miss Westlake.

Miss Westlake Thank you.

Julia (*rising and crossing* L *behind Miss Westlake; thoughtfully*) It just seems a pity she didn't know.

Miss Westlake Didn't know what?

Julia That she was the sacrifice. Might have made it easier if she'd realized it was for the good of the school and all that.

Miss Westlake Oh, I'm sure she did. It was explained very clearly to her.

Julia That's all right then. Put the other girls on their toes, I imagine. Frightened them witless. I should think.

Miss Westlake No, no, certainly not. My girls always regarded me with respect and affection. They knew I had dedicated *Deacons* to their interests alone. To their development as well-educated high-achievers — broad-based and rounded ——

Julia Well, I expect most of them grew out of that.

Miss Westlake Grew out of what?

Julia Being broad-based and rounded. (*She laughs lightly*)

Miss Westlake (*allowing herself to see the joke*) Yes, yes. Puppyfat. Such a problem. Please sit back here beside me, my dear.

Julia sits L *of Miss Westlake*

You really mustn't worry about that girl, you know. She would have been perfectly all right.

Julia You are sure of that?

Miss Westlake She was very pretty, she'd never have any problems. She was too attractive to be down for long. She'd get married ——

Julia But she was not old enough to marry at sixteen.

Miss Westlake Of course not. (*Becoming irritated; her tone sharpens*) She went to another establishment.

Julia Where? What did she do next?

Miss Westlake She went into nursing, I believe.

Julia You're not certain.

Miss Westlake Yes she did. I remember she wrote to the school for a recommendation. Wanted to train in geriatric nursing. Extraordinary.

Julia And you gave her a reference, did you?

Miss Westlake No. Elizabeth Northgate did. It was her responsibility.

Julia Did you see what she wrote about the girl?

Miss Westlake It was average, I suppose.

Julia So she went to Nursing College?

Miss Westlake I'm not sure she did. I think she went on to something else. Maybe didn't stay the pace.

Julia My understanding was that they didn't take her. That she didn't get that recommendation.

Miss Westlake Possibly.

Julia You see, I find it difficult to understand Elizabeth Northgate's action. If she believed in the girl once — then she must have thought she deserved a second chance. Yet she let her down. Why did she turn against her so vindictively?

Miss Westlake I don't know.

Julia Shouldn't she have stood up for her?

Miss Westlake Against me? I don't think so. (*Pause; her manner sweetens*) It is thirty years ago. *Deacons* is no more. I hardly know what happened to most of the staff let alone individual girls.

Julia No, of course not.

Miss Westlake Some keep in touch of course. Most of the girls did very well and their names appear in the newspapers, heading committees, in government office, in academic fields. The younger members of my staff, like Elizabeth Northgate, would have been much in demand.

Julia Didn't you ever wonder what happened to her?

Miss Westlake I know what happened to her.

Julia (*surprised*) You do?

Miss Westlake Oh yes. When *Deacons* was first absorbed she was quite at a loose end ——

Julia No, I was meaning ... go on.

Miss Westlake I had the house my father had lived in. I leased it out for years. Then I moved into it again. Too big for me, so she and I shared it. Ran it as a private crammer for quite a while — very happily — until ... (*She breaks off, then collects herself*) Until, she — she moved on ...

Pause

Julia And you have never worried about Penny Farthing?

Miss Westlake Worry? Why do you say "worry"?

Julia Did you never worry that you might have damaged her — the pair of you.

Miss Westlake The "pair of us"?

Julia You and Elizabeth Northgate between you.

Miss Westlake (*stiffening*) How could you imagine that? What an idea. I told you Elizabeth quite spoiled the girl.

Julia Spoiled her? As in ruined? As in corrupted? Did you ever consider that the girl might hold it against you —when she was older —and understood the world better?

Miss Westlake Life moves on, Miss Griffiths.

Julia (*correcting her*) Griffith…

Miss Westlake I always stressed that to my girls. Move on. Do not waste time looking backwards. We liked to familiarize our girls with sayings from philosophers. Their wise words will serve you all your life. "Never regret your folly. There is folly also in regret." I am sure that maxim stayed with any girl who'd had the benefit of being at *Deacons.*" Even with the Farthing girl. Penny as they all called her. I can't remember what her real Christian name was. What was it?

Julia That seems a pretty empty maxim if I may say so. What else can anyone do?

Miss Westlake Oh, you don't realize ... Many people collapse at life's first blow. Simply lean on others all their days. Never fight their own corner. I pride myself my girls learnt to fight their own corner.

Julia They should have.

Miss Westlake I hope so.

Julia But you never saw her again?

Miss Westlake Who? The Farthing girl? No.

Julia She never sought you out?

Miss Westlake No, why should she?

Julia (*quietly*) Why should she indeed. (*She turns aside*) Not to thank you for anything that's for sure.

Miss Westlake I beg your pardon? My hearing is not so acute as it was. One of the failing faculties of age ... Many of my old girls have visited me, of course. I expect they'll come to call on me here at *Merrywinds.*

Julia If you get in.

Miss Westlake Yes, yes of course.

Julia Do you imagine Penny Farthing will come calling, if she finds out you are here?

Miss Westlake It isn't likely. Why ever should she?

Julia Revenge is sweet.

Miss Westlake Revenge is sweet?

Julia Is that a saying she might know?

Miss Westlake Revenge? How do you mean?

Julia She could hold a grudge. You effectively blocked her getting to university. I'm sure she must have resented that.

Miss Westlake I explained to you ——

Julia She was prevented from getting into Nursing College. Given the opportunity, she might like to get her own back. Don't you know?

Miss Westlake Ah! Ah yes, I think I see what is concerning you. My dear
    woman, if you are worried that this person might turn up at *Merrywinds* and
    create some sort of fracas — I'm perfectly sure she will never discover I've
    moved in here.
Julia If you do.
Miss Westlake Miss Griffiths, as regards ——
Julia "Mrs" ——
Miss Westlake What? This ratification of the Board's decision is purely a
    formality, surely? The Chairman, Dr Redfern, implied that it usually is.
    Your signature, I mean. Surely just a formality? Usually.
Julia Usually, yes.
Miss Westlake "A little chat with the social service manager in charge,"
    they said. "Just so that she can meet you face to face and get to know
    something about you personally. See you are the right type. Just so that she
    can support our decision by putting her signature on the bottom of the
    official acceptance. That is all that is required. And you'll be installed in
    Merrywinds in a couple of months." "That will suit me very admirably",
    I told Dr Redfern, "because I have my house on the market already." It
    really is far too big. Quite a burden. Especially now. I am beginning to need
    a little care and attention. I'm most anxious to get this matter settled, Miss
    Griffiths.
Julia Yes. What would you do if a place at *Merrywinds* is not available to
    you?
Miss Westlake Not available? You mean not at all? But it must be. I am quite
    sure I qualify for the accommodation here.
Julia Qualify?
Miss Westlake I was told so, quite definitely. All it needs is your signature,
    that is all.

Pause

Julia watches the older woman keenly

Of course, if you are not prepared to give it, though I can't imagine why,
    then ——
Julia Then ?
Miss Westlake Then I will have to take it up with a higher authority.
Julia Miss Westlake, as regards *Merrywinds* I am the higher authority. If I
    say you are to be admitted then you are admitted. If I say you are not
    acceptable then you will not be admitted. Is that clear?
Miss Westlake I do not understand all this. What is the problem?
Julia It's quite simple. A little matter of ——

Julia's mobile phone bleeps

Excuse me. (*She rises L to answer the phone*) Yes? … Yes, Bobbie? … Who? … Dr who? … No, Bobbie, not Dr Who. … Very funny, but we've had that joke before. Give me Jill, there's a good lad …. (*Pause*) Jill? What is it? … Dr Redfern. … What message? … About whom? … I see. When was it sent?... Well, where is it then? ...I see. All right …. Yes, well we've had quite an in-depth talk. Sitting here in the sun. I think we both understand each other. So what did Dr Redfern say? … Very well. Thanks Jill.

Pause. Julia tucks the mobile phone into her belt. Miss Westlake smiles to herself

You see, the point is, Miss Westlake, I have to go through your papers and initial all the pages and make my mark in all those little boxes in the questionnaire. Bureaucracy at its best, you know.

Miss Westlake Ah. But at the end of all that you'll accept my application, yes?

Julia (*moving across the front of the stage to* R) You want to come here to *Merrywinds* very much, don't you, Miss Westlake.

Miss Westlake Very much. Very much indeed. I am sure Dr Redfern explained that to you. That was Dr Redfern on your telephone wasn't it?

Julia It was a message from him, yes.

Miss Westlake About my application?

Julia Yes.

Miss Westlake Well, then …

Julia gathers up the folder and clipboard from the chair. She finds the rose, which has now been crushed underneath her folder and clipboard. She picks it up and discards it

Julia (*lightly*) I must go up to the house and track down those papers of yours. Clearly the office staff are involved in some vitally important business which is monopolizing their concentration and creating a serious brain-overload. The holiday roster probably.

Miss Westlake And you'll sign my application, Miss Griffiths.

Julia (*firmly*) It is "Griffith", actually. And "Mrs". (*She flourishes her left hand, and shows her wedding ring*)

Miss Westlake (*not looking at Julia's hand*) Mrs Griffith. I do apologize. I'm getting bad at names.

Julia By the way, Penny Farthing's real Christian name was Julia.

Miss Westlake Oh yes. Now I recall. Julia Farthing. I'm sure she did well enough, you know. So pretty. They always get by, the attractive ones. You need never worry. You'd never forget her. Quite striking colouring. Are you going for my folder?

Julia Shall we go up together?

Miss Westlake Please go ahead, Miss — Mrs Griffith. I'll take a little longer than you.

Julia Very well. I'll see you in the sitting-room.

Miss Westlake It must be about teatime, surely. Four is a civilized hour. I believe the scones here are delicious.

Julia Of global renown.

Miss Westlake Do carry on. I'll follow up the gravel path. (*She stirs stiffly and reaches for her handbag*)

Julia (*moving to her*) You can manage?

Miss Westlake Of course I can. I'm so glad Dr Redfern telephoned. Makes matters easier, doesn't it. Changes things perhaps.

Julia Changes things? Not at all. Dr Redfern was simply sending me his apologies for the late arrival of your file.

Miss Westlake Oh.

Julia I did say, Miss Westlake, that the decision is entirely mine.

Miss Westlake (*weakly*) I had thought Dr Redfern would take my part.

Julia Against me? I don't think so.

Julia starts to exit US

Miss Westlake (*regaining her spirit*) Mrs Griffith! One moment.

Julia stops. She moves back DS

(*Still sitting autocratically erect, facing front*) Something you said. Earlier on. About revenge. It troubles me.

Julia It's just a saying. A quote. Familiar to your pupils, I expect. Revenge is sweet. Isn't that so?

Miss Westlake Very likely. But there is, of course, "a nobler species of revenge" …

Julia "A nobler species of revenge" … ?

Miss Westlake "To have the power of a severe retaliation and not to exercise it". Certainly a true Deacon girl would appreciate that.

Julia Yes. Maybe a true Deacon girl would.

Miss Westlake And do you agree?

Julia hesitates. She looks hard at the older woman

Julia (*nodding*) I'll see you at tea, Miss Westlake.

Julia makes her exit briskly, UL

As soon as Julia has gone, Miss Westlake feels into her handbag and brings out a folding walking stick. She opens it out to its full length

The walking stick is white

Miss Westlake, obviously partially-sighted but determinedly capable, moves off. She exits UR, *in the same direction as Julia*

The CURTAIN *falls*

FURNITURE AND PROPERTY LIST

On stage: Two deckchairs
Windbreak
Folding chair. *On it:* Beach towel and a "Scientific Computing World" magazine
Beachball
A seashell

Off stage: Picnic bag containing a coconut; a soft drink with an attached plastic straw; a tissue and a general assortment of food – including two hard-boiled eggs, a bunch of grapes, bag of bread, a piece of apple, a sandwich (**Doris**)
Picnic bag containing small snack of food, sunglasses and tanning mousse (**Beryl**)
An assortment of trophies won at a fair

On stage: Folding table. *On it*: Small ashtray and a pack of playing cards
Windbreak
Two beach chairs. *On it*: **Deborah**'s cardigan draped on the back of the chair
Stool
Walking stick for **Deborah**
Picnic basket containing a flask, with lemonade; two beakers; a plastic box, filled with biscuits; and a plastic bag
Various deckchairs, sunhats, towels etc.

Off stage: Handbag containing cigarette and a lighter (**Marion**)

On stage: Two beach chairs
Large holdall handbag (**Maggie**)

Off stage: Large holdall handbag containing a wrapped bun, a mobile phone, a diary and a pen (**Pascaline**)

Personal: **Maggie**: spectacles; an assortment of scarves; mobile phone; pencil,
              with a broken lead; notepad with a biro attached; a bag of jelly baby
              sweets

SHORT CHANGED

On stage: Three top-range canvas chairs
              Miss Westlake's large handbag containing a folding white walking
              stick

Personal: **Julia**: clipboard and a folder, containing various papers; mobile phone
              and a rose
              Miss Westlake: handkerchief

LIGHTING PLOT

Day Trippers

To open: Full stage lighting; bright, sunny effect

No cues

The Guilt Card

To open: Full stage lighting; bright sunny effects

No cues

Theatrical Digs

To open: Full stage lighting; bright sunny effect

No cues

Short Changed

To open: Full stage lighting; sunny effect

No cues

EFFECTS PLOT

DAY TRIPPERS

Cue 1:   As the play opens   (Page 1)
Sound of seagulls crying

Cue 2:   **Doris** hesitates   (Page 1)
Fade seagulls as the dialogue begins

Cue 3:   **Beryl**: " ... mind! Not another word!"   (Page 16)
Sound of seagulls crying take over from the voices

THE GUILT CARD

Cue 1:   As the CURTAIN rises   (Page 21)
Sound of waves

Cue 2:   **Marion** enters UR   (Page 21)
Fade wave sound as the dialogue begins

Cue 3:   **Marion** and **Deborah** exit   (Page 35)
Sound of waves crashing on to the beach

THEATRICAL DIGS

Cue 1:   As the CURTAIN rises   (Page 39)
Sound of waves crashing on to the beach

Cue 2:   **Maggie** replaces her spectacles on her nose   (Page 39)
Fade wave sound as the dialogue begins

Cue 3:   **Maggie**: " ... but the point is —— "   (Page 47)
Maggie's *mobile phone beeps*

Cue 4:   **Maggie** answers the phone   (Page 47)
Mobile phone stops beeping as it is answered

Cue 5:   **Pascaline**: " ... cut off! Honestly!"   (Page 49)
The mobile phone in **Pascaline**'s *hand beeps*

Cue 6:	**Pascaline**: " ... Oh no she hasn't."	(Page 49)
	Mobile phone stops beeping as she answers it	
Cue 7:	**Maggie**: " ... wizened skin and —— "	(Page 50)
	Both mobile phones beep	
Cue 8:	Both **Maggie** and **Pascaline** dive to answer the phones	(Page 50)
	Both mobile phones stop beeping as they are answered	

SHORT CHANGED

Cue 1:	**Miss Westlake**: "To make decisions —— "	(Page 59)
	Julia's *mobile phone beeps*	
Cue 2:	**Julia**: "Excuse me a moment."	(Page 59)
	The mobile phone stops beeping as she answers it	
Cue 3:	**Julia**: "A little matter of —— "	(Page 68)
	Julia's *mobile phone beeps*	
Cue 4:	**Julia** *rises* L *to answer the mobile phone*	(Page 69)
	The mobile phone stops beeping as she answers it